D0868610

# THE OTTER SPOTTERS

# A Wildlife Adventure in Alaska

# THE OTTER SPOTTERS

## A Wildlife Adventure in Alaska

### By Judy Swain Garshelis

iUniverse, Inc.
New York   Bloomington

iUniverse books may be ordered through booksellers or by contacting:

iUniverse
1663 Liberty Drive
Bloomington, IN 47403
www.iuniverse.com
1-800-Authors (1-800-288-4677)

ISBN: 978-1-4401-6130-8 (sc)
ISBN: 978-1-4401-6129-2 (ebook)
ISBN: 978-1-4401-6128-5 (dj)

Library of Congress Control Number: 2009932560

Printed in the United States of America

iUniverse rev. date: 8/26/2009

Cover otter photo by Dave Smith
Cover design by Tom Page and Dave Garshelis

# Dedication

For my husband, Dave (I call him Turk), my sons, Daren and Brian, and my parents, Ellie and Walt. Dad died two months after our second field season.

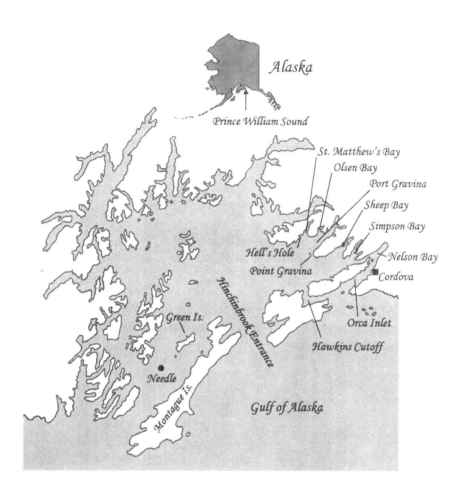

Figure 1. Prince William Sound, Alaska, showing places mentioned in text.

# Contents

# Foreword—How It All Began

*By David Garshelis, PhD*

I clearly recall the day, thirty years ago, when Dr. Don Siniff, Professor of Ecology at the University of Minnesota, offered me a chance to study sea otters in Alaska for my PhD. I had just finished a MS project on black bears, and knew very little about marine mammals, or the sea, for that matter. I managed to obtain a copy of the sea otter "bible" of the time, an extraordinarily comprehensive monograph by Karl Kenyon, based on his study in the Aleutian Islands during 1955–67. My study site would be further east and north (in fact, the most northerly sea otter population), in Prince William Sound.

Kenyon studied otters by observations from shore, by examining dead ones that he shot, and by netting and tagging them when they were hauled out on the beach. One of the limitations of Kenyon's work, and for the several researchers that came after him, was that identifiable individuals could be reobserved only by happenstance, usually when they died and their tag was recovered. In my study, I would have the opportunity to use small radio-transmitters to find individuals virtually at will, and thereby gain greater insights into their life history—at least that was the plan, although no study goes exactly by plan. That's the story that Judy, my wife and resilient field assistant, tells in this book.

Before embarking on a study, there are innumerable preparations: obtaining the equipment, arranging the logistics, and developing a study design by reading and building upon the work of previous investigators. I started by collecting all the literature I could find. At the time, there wasn't much, but it stretched back a long way.

The first recognized study of sea otters was by Georg Wilhelm Steller. Steller was a German naturalist on board a Russian expedition commanded by Vitus Bering, which was directed to search for the enigmatic land now called Alaska. They sailed east from Kamchatka in early June of 1741. Six weeks later, Bering's ship, the *St. Peter*, dropped anchor for the first time, offshore of the new land. They were on the lee side of Kayak Island, just outside the entrance of Prince William Sound.

When the crew went ashore to replenish supplies of fresh water, Steller had his first opportunity to investigate the fauna and flora. As he waded ashore, being the first trained naturalist on Alaskan soil, Steller found the sandy beach speckled with sea otter scats (feces). Running the sun-dried scats through his fingers he would have seen tiny bits of shells from clams, crabs, snails, and maybe some urchins. He commented in his journal that the sheer abundance of these scats was evidence that native people must not hunt sea otters (later studies indicated that Aleuts, native people on the Aleutian islands, did hunt sea otters, sometimes excessively, at various times during their 2500-year history).

Steller was frustrated to be recalled back to the ship after only ten hours of frenzied exploration and discovery (including the Steller's jay). He didn't know then that in four months he would have all the time that he needed to explore another uncharted island and fully employ his naturalist skills. That island, named for the expedition commander, Bering (who died there with much of his crew), lies at the very western edge of the Aleutian chain. The *St. Peter* shipwrecked there in late fall, as they were rushing to return to Kamchatka (less than two hundred miles away) before winter.

The stranded crew, suffering from scurvy, was forced to subsist mainly on sea otter meat.

Steller's observations of sea otter behavior and natural history on Bering Island proved to be remarkably astute and accurate. He recorded their diet, mating, birthing, and pup rearing. In a few respects, though, his information differs from what we know of sea otters today. He suggested, for example, that they were monogamous—240 years later, with the benefits of modern technology, we found this not to be true. Most unexplainably, Steller indicated that he saw them swimming from the ocean up rivers and into fresh water lakes, a behavior characteristic of river otters but not sea otters.

The marooned crew on Bering Island were well aware that sea otters were valuable not only as food, but for their very fine and densely furred pelts. Previously, along the shores of Kamchatka, they were hunted by natives and traded to Russian merchants, who sold them to the Chinese, to trim their clothing. However, otter numbers in Kamchatka were not nearly like those found around Bering Island. Steller and other crew members recognized the potential value of the furs so they killed and collected the pelts from approximately eight hundred otters during their nine-month stay. The otters were initially so unafraid of the human intruders that they could easily be clubbed when they were hauled out on the beach. "They covered the shore in great droves," Steller wrote, "they would come up to our fires and would not be driven away until, after many of them had been slain, they learned to know us and run away." Eventually, most of the otters moved to the far side of the island.

The crew ultimately built a small boat to take them off the island and back to Kamchatka; however, it could not hold all the otter skins that they had collected, so many had to be left behind. Moreover, after setting sail, they found that their makeshift boat badly leaked, so to prevent it from sinking, all unessential cargo had to be thrown overboard—including most of the remaining sea otter skins. One ranking crew member, though, secretly stowed away a stash of pelts under his bunk, which fetched a fine price when they ultimately reached Kamchatka. Word then spread of the multitude of sea otters (as well as foxes, fur seals, and sea cows) at Bering Island, prompting a great rush to reap the bounty.

Fur hunters from Kamchatka began exploiting the westernmost Aleutian Islands. Only fourteen years after Steller left Bering Island, sea otters were reported to be completely exterminated there. Hunters then pushed further eastward through the Aleutians, Alaska Peninsula, Kodiak Island, Prince William Sound, and beyond, returning with hundreds to thousands of pelts, and devastating many sea otter populations in their wake.

In May 1778, Captain James Cook, commanding the *Resolution* and *Discovery*, sailed into Prince William Sound, hoping to find a passageway to the Arctic Ocean (and a route to the Atlantic). He sailed around Green Island (our eventual study site), which he named for its undulating tree-covered hills that were in contrast to the steep, rocky mountains of the larger islands in the sound. Cook commented in the ship's log that the area had numerous small islands and underwater rocks and reefs (which we later learned was ideal habitat for sea otters). During our study we often found it amusing to visualize Cook's two, three-masted ships anchored offshore. A diary from one of Cook's crew noted that they saw "a great number of whales and seal and sea beavers" (sea otters) swimming around their vessels when they anchored between Green and Montague Islands to do repairs. The crew traded with the natives, who arrived in skin-boats full of sea otter pelts (paying as little as one iron nail for one pelt); eventually the pelts would be sold in China (after Cook's death).

Sea otter hunting continued to escalate into the next century, and was, for a time, the largest commercial industry along the Pacific coast. Alexander Baranov, Director of the Russian-American Company (the company that monopolized the sea otter trade), wrote in 1795: "Around Kad'iak Island and in Kenai Bay the sea otters are completely extinct, so I had to sail with all our forces to Chugatsk Bay [Prince William Sound], where there are plenty of them." Ultimately, Russian fur hunters became aware that otter numbers were rapidly diminishing, prompting the Russian-American Company to impose harvest limitations. When the United States bought Alaska in 1867, justified in part by the potential wealth of natural resources, sea otter harvesting resumed, unabated. Even though otter numbers were low at this time, American traders were able to obtain and sell enough sea otter pelts over the next forty years to surpass in value the total purchase price of Alaska. Notably, nearly all the hunting was done by shooting otters in the water, as by this time the animals had learned the dangers of hauling out.

The extraordinary slaughter of sea otters belied the warm feelings that they stirred among naturalists, writers, sailors, and even many hunters, due to their human-like antics. Prolific turn-of-the-century author of outdoors and natural history books, Earnest Thompson Seton, ended his account of the sea otter with these words, "As one reads of its mild and human face, its fish-like hinder parts, its human arms, in which the mother, two-breasted, carries her whimpering babe, and croons it to its slumber, or plays with it, as she sports in the rolling surf, can one not readily believe that in this we have, perhaps, the original of the mermaids and mermen of the ancient tales?"

By 1911, an international treaty to protect declining stocks of fur seals was signed, and somewhat as an afterthought, sea otters were included. However, a wide scale survey at the time indicated that sea otters had already been completely eradicated. Of course, if that had really been the case, we would not have been able to study this magnificent animal, and Judy would not have written this book of our adventures and discoveries.

Gradually, during the 1920s and 1930s, reports began to surface of the existence of a few small pockets of remaining otters on some Aleutian Islands. In 1924, two otters were illegally killed in southwestern Prince William Sound, the first documented evidence that some still persisted there, as well. Several sporadic sightings of otters were recorded in the southwestern portion of the sound during the 1940s and 1950s.

The first thorough sea otter survey in and around Prince William Sound was conducted from an airplane in 1959—about two hundred were found to reside around Kayak Island, where Steller first observed the beach dotted with scats; the largest numbers were seen in the shallow waters between Montague and Green

Islands, where Cook had anchored his two ships. The population continued to recover, and expanded northward into coastal bays that had been vacant of otters for decades, possibly a century.

Dr. Don Siniff began initial studies of sea otters in the northeastern corner of the sound, which had been newly reoccupied by otters, in 1977. The initial focus of that work was to study the potential effects of an oil spill, as the pipeline carrying Prudhoe Bay crude from the North Slope to Valdez had just been completed, and there was fear of a spill sometime in the future (of course that came to be true in 1989 when the *Exxon Valdez* ran aground on a reef named for William Bligh, sailing master on Cook's expedition). Don asked me to continue this work, and expand it as I saw fit for my dissertation.

With Judy's most able and painstaking help, we did just that. It is now a thrill to relive that experience through her colorful writing, extracted from her detailed field notes (which I have to admit, I gave her endless grief about at the time). I hope the reader of this account of our work will gain an appreciation for the amount of effort it takes to learn just a small bit about the animals that share the Earth with us.

# References

Berkh, V.N. 1974. A chronological history of the discovery of the Aleutian Islands or the exploits of Russian merchants, with a supplement of historical data on the fur trade. Translated by D. Krenov. Kingston, Ontario: Limestone Press.

Cook, J. 1784. *A voyage to the Pacific Ocean. Undertaken by the command of his majesty, for making discoveries in the northern hemisphere. To determine the position and extent of the west side of North America; its distance from Asia; and the practicality of a northern passage to Europe.* London: Order of the Lords Commissioners of the Admiralty.

Ford, C. 1998. *Where the sea breaks its back. The epic story of early naturalist Georg Steller and the Russian exploration of Alaska.* Anchorage: Alaska Northwest Books. (Orig. pub. 1966).

Kenyon, K. W. 1969. The sea otter in the Eastern Pacific Ocean. *North American Fauna* 68:1–352.

Lensink, C. J. 1962. The history and status of sea otters in Alaska. PhD diss., Purdue University.

Seton, E.T. 1929. *Lives of game animals.* Vol. II, Part II. Garden City: Doubleday and Doran and Co.

Steller, G. W. 1899. De bestiis marinis [The beasts of the sea]. Translated by W. Miller and J.E. Miller. In *Fur seals and fur seal islands of the North Pacific Ocean.* Part III, 179–218. Washington: U.S. Government Printing Office. (Orig. pub. 1751).

# Preface

This book recounts the true story of two people studying sea otters in Alaska. My husband, Turk, and I went to Prince William Sound, Alaska in 1980 and 1981 to conduct research on the social organization, feeding habits, movement patterns, and breeding behavior of sea otters. Turk was a PhD candidate at the University of Minnesota in wildlife biology. His advisor, Dr. Don Siniff, felt strongly that our marriage would not survive if I were Turk's field assistant; the challenges of a field study can put a lot of strain on personal relationships. However, when Turk told him we were going to work together, Don supported it. I was a public health nurse in Minneapolis and was able to take a leave of absence from my job in order to do this.

Turk and I worked together on this study for six months a year, two years in a row, and Turk also went back to Alaska for shorter trips during the winter. We each wrote field notes on a daily basis under the light of a Coleman lantern in a tent or cabin. I frequently teased Turk, saying my notes would become the basis for an interesting book someday, because they were very detailed about everything that happened to us and also described our emotions. Turk's notes were very scientific about the otters (always listed them by number and not name), and only briefly mentioned the dangerous situations that we encountered.

I planned on writing the book after retirement, when I had

more time, but in the summer of 2007 I had the opportunity to return to Prince William Sound and help conduct counts of sea otters. We had a day to return to Green Island, our former study site, and found many things exactly as they had been twenty-seven years before. The beaches were the same, the smells were the same (and very unique to Green Island), females with pups were in many of the same places, and territorial males had the same territories! The cabin that we stayed in, however, had been burned down by the U.S. Forest Service and a new, much fancier one, had been built a short distance from the previous site. Many memories flooded into my head and I was overwhelmed with emotion. I knew that I could not wait any longer to write this story. I wanted our children to know about our very unique Alaskan adventure. I also hope that you, the reader, will find this account of our quest to understand sea otters as interesting and inspiring as it was living it.

# Acknowledgments

I give a very special thanks to the following people for helping with this project. Dr. Don Siniff, professor from the University of Minnesota (presently retired), and Turk's advisor, allowed me to work as Turk's field assistant, even though he did not initially think it was a good idea. We always enjoyed his visits to the field. He also provided guidance, friendship, and funding for this project.

Ancel Johnson, sea otter biologist for the U.S. Fish and Wildlife Service (presently retired), gave us an incredible amount of logistical support and friendship. Ancel spent hours with us discussing sea otters, let us use his boats and other equipment, and allowed us to stay in the cabin he built on Green Island.

Dick and Kay Groff "took us under their wing" and helped on innumerable occasions. Dick was always there for us in an emergency. Dick and Kay also invited us to their home for dinner several times and allowed Turk to stay with them during the winter. We developed a long lasting friendship.

A big thanks goes to my good friend, Tom Gulya, for spending several hours editing the manuscript.

The biggest gratitude, however, goes to Turk, my husband, for spending numerous hours editing this book, and for providing me the opportunity to be his field assistant on this project. We had always been close, but this project made us even closer. We learned to work side by side on a daily basis in some difficult field situations. Turk always treated me as an equal partner and researcher. I cannot thank him enough for giving me this once in a lifetime experience.

# Starting Our Field Study

"Stick with me and you will have a lot of firsts." That is what Turk said to me after he asked me to marry him. He had no idea how true this statement would be, for both of us. One of these "firsts" occurred in July 2007. I found myself, with Turk, in a fifteen-foot rubber boat (Zodiac) … in the ocean … in Alaska … conducting counts of sea otters. As we slowed down the motor to go over the wake from a large boat, the water suddenly seemed to part and a humpback whale lurched vertically in front of us. Its eye stared at us as it rose and then slammed its head back into the water. The splash created two-foot waves, and our Zodiac spun sideways as it tilted forty-five degrees. As I quickly grabbed a rope on the side of the boat, my body slid toward the water. My heart was pounding and it was hard to catch a breath. We did not dare move the boat for fear of the whale coming up under us and knocking us into the water. The whale definitely was aware of our location. The waves settled down and my heart eventually started to beat in a normal rhythm. I should have known that we could not be in Prince William Sound without having a close call. These types of experiences occurred on a regular basis when we studied sea otters in 1980 and 1981.

May 1980

My husband, Turk, and I went to Prince William Sound, Alaska to study sea otters for Turk's PhD project in wildlife biology through the University of Minnesota. Prince William Sound (see fig. 1, preceding Contents page) is located in south-central Alaska, about 290 miles southeast of Anchorage and is home to the northernmost population of sea otters. Sea otters range east to the Alaskan panhandle, southward to British Columbia and California, and west to Kodiak Island, the Aleutian Islands, and Russia.

On May 9 we arrived in Cordova, Alaska, a small fishing town with a population slightly over two thousand, mainly men. From a distance the town looks quaint and colorful. Closer up, it takes on a more disheveled appearance with lots of bars, peeling paint on most of the buildings, upside down signs, and potholes in all of the three main roads. Everyone in the town walked around in rubber boots and raincoats.

Turk and I planned to catch sea otters and study their social organization, breeding behavior, feeding habits, and movements. To help us get started, another student, Sheridan, came to help us.

Prior to our arrival we had purchased a twelve-foot trailer, sight unseen, to live in when we would not be in our field camp. The previous owner of the trailer, Betty, met us at the Cordova airport and took us to the trailer, which was parked at a U.S. Forest Service warehouse. We went to all the trailer courts in Cordova looking for a site to keep the trailer, but none had vacancies. Betty then introduced us to the district Forest Service ranger in Cordova, Dick Groff, and we explained our predicament. Dick allowed us to temporarily hook the trailer up to the Forest Service warehouse. Later that day, as we attached the water supply to the trailer, water gushed out all over the floor. This was the start of our first Alaskan adventure—calamities, annoyances, and dangerous situations mixed with wonderful people and thrilling discoveries about a fascinating animal.

The following day we started preparing for our study of sea otters. We had previously been given permission to use two skiffs, seventeen-foot Boston Whalers, from Ancel Johnson, the U.S. Fish and Wildlife Service sea otter biologist in Anchorage. The boats were tied up at the Forest Service dock in the Cordova harbor. We climbed into one boat and headed to Simpson Bay (fig. 1), a forty-five minute boat ride from Cordova, to look at last year's campsite. We had been there for two months the previous summer with some other University of Minnesota students and Turk's advisor, Dr. Don Siniff, to scope out the feasibility of this study, to work out some research methods, and, most importantly, to have Don show us how to catch otters. We planned to use this same campsite for our study.

When we got to the campsite, the platform that we had built for our tent was still intact, but missing a few boards. As we looked around Simpson Bay we saw nine sea otters. Some of them were resting on their backs while others were feeding. As we drove the boat back to Cordova for more supplies, the motor quit working. After fifteen minutes of cleaning spark plugs, it started again. Since we were totally reliant on this boat as our only means of transportation around Prince William Sound, we hoped this was not a bad omen.

A few days later we bought lumber and other camp supplies in Cordova and went to the Eyak Native American Corporation to obtain a permit to camp on their land in Simpson Bay. We left for Simpson Bay in mid-afternoon and took both Boston Whalers filled with equipment and supplies. Immediately we ran into trouble. One of the motors kept sputtering and stalling, but this was quickly fixed by changing gas cans. We were hoping to take the boats to a warehouse in Olsen Bay to get other camping and trapping supplies, but the water was too rough. On a good day, Olsen Bay is a fifty-minute boat ride from Simpson Bay (fig. 1). Today, with the wavy seas and rough-running boat, it seemed wise to stay in Simpson Bay and look for otters. Last year there had been over sixty otters living in this bay, but now we only saw three. Where had they gone? Finding them would be our first challenge.

The next day, Sheridan and I searched around Simpson Bay again while Turk took the other boat to Nelson Bay, which is further east. We only saw scattered otters, and the biggest group was three. We met in Simpson Bay for lunch and decided to search westward in Sheep Bay. In Sheep Bay we also walked along the beach looking for carcasses of otters that died during the winter, and scats (feces).

Winter storms are a source of sea otter mortality, and in rough weather sea otters often come ashore to rest, and die.

Since there are both brown and black bears in Prince William Sound, I wore a cowbell on one of my hip boots to make noise while I walked. Some say the sound frightens bears away, while other "authorities" (or jokesters) say it serves as a dinner bell! I also carried a rifle just in case. Sheridan gave me a crash course during lunch on how to shoot. My aim was terrible and I knew I would be in trouble if I had to shoot for real. As I walked the beach I saw two bald eagles flying close together and calling to each other and another one sitting on a nest in a tree. While the scenery was beautiful and wildlife wonderful, none of us found any sea otter carcasses on the beach. We also did not see any otters in Sheep Bay. Discouraged, we headed back to Simpson Bay where we had left the second boat. To add to our frustration, the boat motor refused to start. After twenty minutes of trying various ways to get it started, we suddenly noticed two wires hanging loose under the console. They had apparently come apart when we loaded equipment into the boat earlier in the day. We connected the wires and, with much relief, it started. We arrived back to Cordova at 7:00 PM, three hours before dark. Turk used a payphone to call Ancel, the sea otter biologist, to seek his advice on where the otters might be living. He suggested Port Gravina, one bay west of Sheep Bay.

The next day it was raining hard, but we took one of the Whalers to Port Gravina to look for otters. We saw thirteen sea otters in one of the bays, but as we searched in another bay, called Hell's Hole, we came to realize the source of the bay's name. With no warning, the water turned from calm, to choppy, and then to curling whitecaps. It was all we could do to keep the boat from getting tossed onto the beach. We struggled against the incoming tide, which was pouring through the single narrow mouth of this bay, hoping our motor wouldn't quit. Finally, getting out of Hell's Hole, we decided to head straight back to Cordova. The waves in Port Gravina were three feet high, the wind was very strong and in our face, and the rain was pelting. The boat, while a good workhorse, was not the picture of comfort. It didn't even have a windshield, and with only a hard wooden bench seat, it was better to stand when the water got rough, so you could absorb the constant shock of the pounding waves with your knees. It took two and one-half hours to get back, twice the normal amount of time for the trip. We were chilled, soaked to the bone, and discouraged again.

The next morning the rain had stopped, it was overcast, fifty degrees (Fahrenheit), and calm. We decided, in desperation, to check Nelson Bay again. We knew that the otter population in Prince William Sound had been expanding. Otters had been decimated in the fur trade during the 1800s throughout Alaska, and barely survived in a small area of southwest Prince William Sound, where, in 1911, they were first protected by an international treaty. From this small, isolated population, they slowly expanded. Ancel and Don had seen them in Port Gravina in 1974, in Sheep Bay in 1977, and we saw them in Simpson Bay in 1979. Hopefully, they continued their progression to Nelson Bay, but Turk had looked there a few days ago and only saw a few otters.

As we headed into Nelson Bay, going very slowly, we saw a large clump of brown in the center like a large massive raft on the water. It was undulating in the light breeze. As we got closer, we noticed that it was actually a group of sea otters all resting together; indeed what scientists call a "raft." The raft consisted of 120 sea otters—a breakthrough at last! We threw in the anchor so we could stay in one place, watch otters, and take in the excitement. Suddenly, the anchor line broke—a small mishap given the circumstances.

It was apparent that we should set up our camp in Nelson Bay. We drove along the shore and looked for a flat site. Nelson Bay is approximately six miles long and three miles wide, and is surrounded by steep mountains that come right to the water, with waterfalls pouring down from ice caps. Near the back of the bay is a large mudflat at the mouth of a river. While it was nice and flat, the area floods at high tide, so certainly was not a place to camp. Near there, though, was a waterfall running down the side of a huge mountain, which leveled out and became a stream that flowed into the bay. Near the leveled out area there was a grassy knoll on one side of the stream, a perfect place to set up a camp. On the other side of the stream there was a large rocky beach.

We got up at 5:00 AM the next morning to go to Olsen Bay to

get the camping gear and otter-catching nets from the warehouse. When we tried to start one boat, however, the battery was dead. We had the second boat, so we used its battery to jump the dead battery and, for the moment, had two working boats! The water was flat calm so we were able to travel fast. Forty minutes into the trip, in Sheep Bay, the second boat suddenly stopped. None of us knew much about outboard motors, and, until last year, none of us had even driven a boat. With each turn of the key the starter cranked, but the motor would not start. We remembered that last year when a similar thing happened, Don showed us an old trick. He put some "Blazo" (white gas) on the spark plugs because it is more flammable than regular gas. We tried this once, then twice, and finally after the third time and over a half hour of frustration, the boat finally started. Then, after hopping back into the first boat, Turk turned the key and found that the battery was dead again. Luckily, we were again able to jump batteries and continue to Olsen Bay—with both boats.

Thirty minutes later we arrived at the warehouse, a faded green, tin, twelve-by-twelve-foot building owned by the National Marine Fishery Service. It had previously been used to store gear for fish research and management projects. Further back into Olsen Bay, there was a dilapidated wooden research station composed of small bunk buildings and a kitchen. In its heyday, this was a busy place with people monitoring the large run of spawning salmon coming up the river.

We searched through piles of gear and nets, decided what was needed, and piled everything into the two boats. We switched boat batteries so that the dead battery would get charged in the other boat, and put Blazo on the spark plugs in both boats. When we started to drive back toward Cordova the waves were considerably larger and the wind was blowing from the east, which meant it would be in our faces all the way back.

Sheridan was in one boat and Turk and I were in the other. Our boat was overloaded with gear so it was riding low in the water and the waves were breaking over the bow, filling the boat with water. I was standing while driving the boat, trying to keep my balance each time we surged over the top of one wave and plunged into the trough of the next one. Turk found a bucket and bailed water out with one hand as he held onto the side railing with the other to keep from falling out. I remember Turk shouting over the noise of the crashing waves and driving rain, "If the motor quits now we'll get washed up on that boulder beach and die." My heart was pounding and I remember thinking that his voiced pessimism was not helping the situation. I also began wondering if I would ever see my parents again. I guess this was one of those firsts that Turk promised me and I hoped it wasn't also a "last." In the meantime, Sheridan's boat, which was not so overloaded, was taking the waves much better. Eventually, the white-knuckle ride ended when we came into Nelson Bay where it was much calmer. We unloaded the gear at the campsite and returned to Cordova. Turk's description of this day in his field notes simply state, "Judy and I took in a lot of water as our boat ploughed into the waves. Slow trip back to Cordova." His notes were always oddly brief whenever something dangerous happened to us, yet extremely detailed when he wrote about the otters.

The following day it rained too hard to do any work on the water, so we decided to work on the pipes in the trailer, and in the evening, Turk reviewed the sea otter budget. We had $11,000 to spend on this field season and had already spent over $700 in one week for groceries, gas, and motor repairs. We tried to think of ways to cut back on our spending, but had already suffered the consequences of buying cheap rain gear. I had a rip in one leg and the jacket zipper already had two loose teeth. Rain gear in this climate was essential and I was going to need an upgrade in the near future. We also recognized that the binoculars that we brought to Alaska were not adequate because they fogged too easily and took days to dry out. It would cost us several hundred dollars to get a better pair.

The next day it poured rain again, with gale force winds, and ten-foot swells. We did not dare take the boats in the water so we decided to make final preparations for catching otters. Prior to coming to Alaska, Turk had worked with a company in Minnesota to make radio-transmitters, which we planned to attach to a rear flipper of each otter. Because the otters spend a lot of time floating on the surface of the water, we wanted to be able to identify individuals by sight, as well as by radiotracking. Our rainy day project was, thus, painting the radio-transmitters in unique colored patterns. As the rain pounded on the tin roof of the trailer, we joked about our artistic expressions manifested in the designs on the transmitters.

Over the next two days we went back to Nelson Bay and built a tent platform and frame. We put a ten-by-ten-foot wall tent over the frame, set up cots for our sleeping bags, built a small table for the Coleman stove, and unpacked and organized the supplies. Then we had to deal with the issue of anchoring the boat. Tides in Prince William Sound vary by as much as eighteen feet so if the boat were anchored near shore it would be high and dry at low tide and inaccessible at high tide. We solved this problem by setting an anchor with a buoy about one hundred feet from shore. On the buoy was an "O" ring. A long loop of rope went through the ring and all the way to the shore, where it was tied to a tree. A quick-release clip attached the boat to the rope. By pulling the rope one way the boat would go out to the buoy; by pulling in the other direction, the boat came to shore. As long as the water under the buoy was deep enough, the boat would not get beached even at the lowest tides.

Once camp was set up we went to Cordova to the post office to pick up otter immobilizing drugs that were sent to us by a veterinarian in California. The next day we went back to the Olsen Bay warehouse and picked up two otter-catching nets. The nets were modified fishing gill nets that measured three hundred feet long and hung down seventeen feet in the water. A series of eight-inch corks suspended the top of each net, and the bottom had a heavy "lead line" to keep it vertical in the water. This time we made it back to the Nelson Bay camp without boat problems or big waves!

That evening, Turk found a large fresh bear scat on the beach adjacent to our camp. I figured I should get more serious about target practice with the rifle in case I had to defend myself from a bear. Turk and Sheridan made a target out of cardboard and we each practiced shooting the rifle. It was hard to adjust to the kickback of the .30-06 (thirty-aught-six), but I actually hit the target three times. I wondered though, if a 30 percent hit rate would do me any good if I actually encountered a bear. I figured I would put more trust in my cowbell than the rifle. After target practice we saw three large rafts of sea otters in the water directly in front of our camp and got very excited about the prospect of trapping otters and actually starting the study.

The next day we set two nets in Nelson Bay. One end of the net was attached to an anchor and tossed overboard. We then slowly backed up the boat as we guided the lead line and cork line into the water. At one point, the propeller of the boat got caught in a net and it took almost an hour to get it out. Later in the day, feeling optimistic that we were going to catch otters, we mounted an antenna to a ten-foot pole and attached it to one of the boats to allow us to radiotrack otters.

The following morning, Turk checked the nets at 4:00 AM and found that no otters had been caught. However, twenty minutes later he watched an otter swim on its back directly into the net. The nets were not baited in any way so we had to rely on otters swimming into them inadvertently. Upon contacting the cork line, an otter would dive to get under it and then get caught in the net. The lead line was not heavy enough to keep an otter from surfacing, so it could float up and rest.

We approached the otter in the boat, grabbed the hind flippers, and pulled it up to the side of the boat. I leaned over and injected it with the tranquilizer. It took five minutes for the otter to go to sleep. We then pulled him into the boat and extricated him from the net. We pulled him through a five-gallon bucket that had the bottom cut out. That way, while we were working to attach the radio-transmitter to his hind flipper, he could not bite us if he woke up. The drugs we were using (a combination of fentanyl and azaparone) were still experimental at this time so we were uncertain about how long and how deeply the otters would be tranquilized.

We took a moment to examine him closely. It was a young male. He had a torpedo-shaped brown head, a wide neck, long body, and a long flattened tail. His fur was thick, soft, and luxuriant; in fact it is the densest fur of any living mammal, which explains why otters had been so heavily hunted. We each rubbed his fur and noticed that it came out easily and stuck to our wet hands. It was wet on the outside but still dry close to his skin. His skin was so loose you could virtually twist it from one armpit to the other. There was almost no subcutaneous fat. His front paws were like small mittens with tiny claws that had five little digits inside. The hind flippers were thinly covered with hair, and also had five digits, with the largest digit on the outside. In contrast to the tiny front paws, they were broad, webbed, and eight inches long. His ears were only an inch long and he had drooping whiskers. From his nose to the tip of his tail he measured forty-seven inches, of which eleven inches was his tail, and he weighed fifty-two pounds. We took his temperature and pulse and pulled a tiny vestigial premolar. Later in the lab these premolars would be sectioned and the otters' ages would be determined from annular growth rings. We attached two red tags on one hind flipper and a red radio-transmitter on the other, and gave him the obvious name, "Triple Red."

Turk wanted to take him to Simpson Bay, release him, and monitor his movements. He thought it would be an interesting experiment since the otters in Nelson Bay presumably came from Simpson Bay within the last year. Would the otter come directly back to Nelson Bay? If so, how long would it take? Or, did they all come in one big group so an individual may not know the way, like a migrating bird without the flock? We placed the otter in a three-foot cube-shaped wooden crate in the boat and sped off to Simpson Bay. When we arrived there, the otter was awake and its transmitter had come off in the box! After drugging it again, we realized that the transmitter attachment design needed some modification. We reaffixed it using some larger washers under the bolt heads. The otter started to wake up in fifteen minutes so we put him over bow of the boat with his head toward the water. He dove in, but did not act normally. He floated on his back, slowly turned over on his stomach as he put his head underwater, and then proceeded to swim directly into the side of the boat. He appeared to still be sedated so we thought we would give him more antidote to the tranquilizing drug. When we got close to him, he had other thoughts and swam away very fast. We hoped that future captures and handlings would go smoother but we were happy to have the first transmittered otter in our study.

We radiotracked Triple Red for an hour and then lost the signal. We took the boat to the back of Simpson Bay looking for him. He was not there, but we saw a huge black bear walking casually along the beach. Not hearing the radio-signal, we headed back toward Nelson Bay, but had an uneasy feeling that the transmitter may have fallen off the flipper and sunk to the bottom of the ocean. Radio-signals are highly attenuated by salt water so if the transmitter's antenna was a few inches under the water the signal could not be heard. En route to camp we continued to listen for his signal and suddenly picked it up just outside Simpson Bay, and eventually saw him feeding. Each time he dove for one to two minutes the signal could not be heard. With a sigh of relief, we drove back to Nelson Bay to untangle the net, which was in a big ball from the capture of the otter. That task alone took over an hour.

As a marine mammal, sea otters are a federally protected species. We had permits from both the U.S. Fish and Wildlife Service and the state of Alaska, which mandated that we check our nets three times a day. So at 10:30 PM, just before dark, Turk, Sheridan, and I went out to check the nets again. As we approached, we saw several brown blobs in one net and one big brown blob in the other. As we got closer to the first net we found six entangled otters. Three otters were caught in the same spot so we had to act fast. I quickly drew up the drug in a syringe and Turk grabbed one of the otter's hind flippers so I could inject it in the buttocks. Then Turk grabbed a second otter as I drew up more of the drug and injected it, too. Our exhilaration was suddenly quelled when we realized that the third otter in that clump was dead. We pulled it into the boat. He was small, only thirty-six pounds, and had apparently drowned because he was caught so close to the two larger otters. Our hearts sank and we felt sick. However, we could not spend time feeling bad right now because we had a lot of work in front of us. When the two drugged otters were asleep, we pulled them into the boat. We pulled one of them through the bucket and tied the second one in a cargo net. We could not work them up immediately because two other otters were fighting further down the net. We grabbed the net and pulled the boat up to the fighting otters. Sheridan grabbed a paddle that was in the boat and tried to put it between the two otters to keep them from biting each other. I drew up more drugs in a syringe and Turk grabbed one of the otter's hind flippers to hold him still while I drugged it. The otter tried to twist in the net to bite Turk. Sheridan kept the paddle between the two otters until I could drug the other fighting otter. This otter was quite aggressive and it took awhile to get him drugged.

When the drug took effect, we pulled one of the otters on board and put him in the wooden crate. We pulled the other one onto the bow and left him in the tangled net. We now had four drugged otters in the boat (along with the small dead one), and little time to collect data and put on the transmitters before they would wake up. Using our "vast experience" of handling Triple Red that morning, we set out to process these four otters as quickly and orderly as possible. On one hand, we were tempted to skip collecting some of the data and just attach the transmitters, but we knew we would regret it later. We forced ourselves to fill in all the blanks on the data sheets even though it was getting dark and we were working under the light of our flashlights in the pouring rain. Fortunately, the otters cooperated and slept longer than we had anticipated.

When we finished working up the otters, I injected each one with Narcan, the antidote to the tranquilizing drugs. The first otter woke up quickly, dove from the bow of the boat, and swam away. The second otter walked around the bow of the boat and was very mellow, letting us rub his stomach and back. He stayed on the bow for fifteen minutes before diving into the water. The other two otters took longer to wake up. After releasing them, there was still one more otter to deal with in this net. We were able to drug him without difficulty and worked him up without any problems. Then we drove the boat to the second net and worked up the last otter.

Six of the seven otters caught weighed from fifty-one to fifty-six pounds. The seventh otter was the small one that died; we estimated that it was only one-year-old. All the otters were males and had dark brown heads, indicating that they were young. As otters age, their head color becomes whiter.

We finished working up the last otter at 6:00 AM. We were exhausted and felt horrible about the dead otter, which would have to be reported under our permits. We went back to camp, washed up, and prepared to drive to Cordova to call Don and tell him about the dead otter. As our luck, or lack of luck would have it, neither boat would start. Now we had been up all night, had a dead sea otter, and two dead boat motors. We pulled out the spark plugs, put on the magic Blazo, wiped off the battery connections, checked various wires, and after an hour managed to get one boat started.

We arrived in Cordova at 9:00 AM and called Don. He was very understanding and did not think the mortality would jeopardize our permits to catch more otters. We then submitted the necessary reports, went to the trailer, and slept for a blissful seven hours. After supper we took the boat back to Nelson Bay for the evening net check. This time we were happy *not* to see any brown blobs in the nets. My, how our expectations had changed! The nets were extremely tangled and were not hanging down into the water so it would have been unlikely to catch an otter.

We went back to camp and discussed our observations from this past week. We noticed that all the otters that were caught had dark brown heads and were small, yet we had seen solitary otters in Simpson Bay and Sheep Bay that had white heads. Why were all the young dark headed otters in Nelson Bay and the older solitary otters in Simpson and Sheep Bays?

The next morning there were no otters in the nets at 6:00 AM, so we spent the morning radiotracking. We dialed an otter's individual frequency into a receiver, which was wired to the antenna mounted in the boat. The antenna was rotated until we could hear the "beep-beep" signal from the transmitter. We drove the boat in the direction of the loudest signal and approached until we could see the otter swimming, feeding, or resting. By late morning otters were starting to form rafts and we saw a raft of eighty otters, forty of them had white heads. That meant that our initial capture sample of otters was biased toward young otters and that there were older otters also living in Nelson Bay.

After radiotracking we went to Cordova to do errands. When we tried to return to camp, the boat would not start and neither would the small back up motor. We had access to another small motor and put it on the boat and eventually got the main motor started and headed to Nelson Bay. We realized that our research, as well as our safety, would be compromised unless we solved these boat problems, so we made plans to talk to a mechanic as soon as possible. Upon arriving back in Nelson Bay we still had nets to untangle. This was a task that was difficult to do in the water so we loaded them in the boat, one at a time, and hauled them onto the beach.

The next morning we did a necropsy (autopsy) on the dead otter, which took four hours because we measured and weighed each organ. The lungs had water in them, indicating that the otter had drowned. The intestines contained several half-inch worms.

After lunch we drove both boats back to Cordova, where our first priority was to find the outboard motor shop and talk to the mechanic about all of our problems. He was extremely helpful. He explained what was wrong with the ignition in one boat, knew that the other boat was idling too slow, which caused it to stall when in gear, and told us how to fix the problems. He did not know, however, why the battery was draining. While we were working on the boats at the dock a friend from the Forest Service came by and told us to call someone who knew a lot about boats. This second Good Samaritan came down and found a blown fuse on the back of the motor, so we finally had two working boats.

The next day it was overcast until late afternoon and then rained, as usual. By this time I had already gone through two pairs of rain pants and one raincoat. Our plans were to set up an automatic radiotracking station to gather activity data. Turk climbed a one hundred-foot Sitka spruce tree and mounted two antennas to branches pointing in different directions. A cable ran from each antenna to a receiver on the ground. The receiver was programmed to scan the frequencies of the otters, and was connected to an event recorder. Nowadays, scientists record such data digitally, but in those days the only means of recording signals from the receiver was with paper and ink. The event recorder had paper that unwound from one spool onto another, and was marked by small pens with red liquid ink. When the receiver detected a radio-signal, it triggered the corresponding ink pen to move and mark the paper. The paper had printed time gradations so the markings of the pen matched the time of day. If otters were within the detection distance of the receiver, their signal would be recorded twenty-four hours a day. We could determine if the otters were resting or feeding by the pattern of ink marks on the paper. If an otter was resting, the marks on the paper were continuous, whereas if the otter was feeding the pattern would be interrupted each time the otter dove.

We radiotracked later in the day and then untangled the nets on the beach. It was a tedious job and we each developed our own preferred method of untangling it. We worked for over two hours to finish the job.

At low tide the next morning we thought we would try clamming since I had grown up on Cape Cod and considered myself an old hand at this. We went to the mudflat at the back of Nelson Bay. All we dug up were fat innkeepers—a thick, fleshy, worm-like organism. They were three inches long, nearly one inch wide, and were full of clear fluid—too disgusting to eat. It poured all day.

At 8:00 PM we caught a male otter. After drugging him, collecting the data, and putting on a transmitter, we drove the boat to Simpson Bay to release him. We continually tracked him through the night and he returned to Nelson Bay by 4:00 AM! He had traveled seven miles in six hours. Obviously, the otters knew which bays they were in and where they wanted to be.

We went to bed after breakfast following the all night tracking session but Sheridan woke us up at noon. He told us there were thirteen otters in two nets! We had seven otters in one net and six in the other. We had to break up a lot of fights and gave a penicillin shot to two otters because their noses were bleeding from fighting. We were nervous that if another otter died our permits could be revoked. Fortunately, all the otters were fine because Sheridan found them in the net shortly after they were captured. Sheridan got bitten in his arm by one of the drugged otters that temporarily woke up, but it did not puncture the skin through his several layers of clothing.

We drove two otters to Simpson Bay, released them, and tracked them until 4:00 AM. Although it started to get dark at 10:00 PM, it was darkest from 11:00 PM–1:00 AM, but was never pitch black and we could see well enough to navigate the boat. By 4:00 AM it was totally light, giving us sixteen to eighteen hours a day to work in.

The next day we checked the automatic tracking station and all the otters that we had taken to other bays (transplanted) had come back to Nelson Bay. It was so exciting that the tracking station captured this data. It was a nice sunny day so we pulled the nets out of the water to untangle them on the beach. Although we worked on them for hours, we did not get very far. This was the monotonous, tedious, unglamorous part of sea otter research. We joked about hiring a net-picker, or inventing a machine that could do it.

The next day we radiotracked otters on the way to Cordova to buy groceries and supplies and heard a signal very close to town, in Orca Inlet (fig. 1). It was a steady signal, which meant that the otter was not going underwater. Being paranoid about our permits, we jumped to the assumption that it was a dead otter floating on the surface. We drove the boat toward the signal and eventually saw two otters resting together, one of which was the one we were tracking. In fact, it was one of the otters that we had taken to Simpson Bay two nights before. It was clear that otters knew their way around this part of northeastern Prince William Sound.

Back in Nelson Bay, we saw two more otters with transmitters. We could identify them through binoculars by looking at their flippers and seeing the color of their flipper tags and painted transmitters. We also saw a large raft of otters, so we turned off the motor and drifted toward them. As we got closer, some of the otters were unaware of our presence, some were nervous and swam away, and others were curious and approached us. They would dive in the water and pop up within fifteen feet of the boat. They raised their heads and upper body high out of the water (called "periscoping") to look at us. They frequently looked around to be sure other companions were still nearby. This was our first opportunity to photograph this behavior.

The next day Turk and Sheridan brought the starter from one boat to the outboard motor shop in Cordova. I stayed at camp and untangled nets (a woman's work is never done!) and checked the automatic tracking station. In mid-afternoon, a raft of thirty-five otters was resting near the boat mooring. From the beach I was able to identify three of our transmittered otters. As I watched the raft, I noticed that the otters weren't just resting. Many of them were grooming themselves by rubbing their fur and blowing air into it. Others were doing slow somersaults, while still others were playing together or wrestling with each other. As they became aware of me, several began to periscope. Apparently, they do this to get a better view. Sometimes one otter would hold onto another from behind the shoulders, both of them periscoping. It looked as if the rear otter was afraid and was using the front otter as a shield.

As I stood on the beach I became overwhelmed with the sense of how lucky I was to be here. I was surrounded by beautiful mountains, lush, green vegetation that appeared mystically draped with hanging moss, and the ever-changing ocean. The water in the back of Nelson Bay was turbid from the glacial silt coming from the mountains, and after a hard rain it became milky from the increased glacial runoff. Some days the water was so flat you could see reflections of the mountains in it and other days there were whitecaps pounding the beach. To me, the salty air was refreshing. Just behind me the air smelled like damp moss, an association I will always make with the temperate rain forest. The beach in front of me was rocky and slippery with kelp and mussels, not at all like the sandy beaches of Cape Cod where I grew up. Most days we saw few or no people, and we were surrounded by beautiful wildlife. Bald eagles and sea birds were everywhere. We picked a great place to study sea otters! In just twenty-four days, after an ominous start, we had set up camp and an automatic tracking station, caught twenty-two sea otters, transplanted many of them, and monitored their movements. And Turk was happy that "the data was rolling in."

Net for catching otters

Several otters caught in net

Otter caught in net

Drugging an otter in the net

Working up an otter in the boat

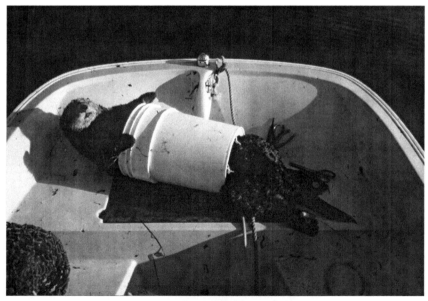

Bucket to keep otters from biting us

Campsite in Nelson Bay

Periscoping otter

Triple Red

Walking beach with rifle

Radiotracking from boat

Large raft of otters

# Mishap In Sheep Bay

*"Hell of a long day for no otter sign found"*
*—excerpt from Turk's field notes*

Part of Turk's study included walking the beaches along the coasts of the different bays looking for otter skulls, bones, and scats. We went to Sheep Bay to spend a full day walking the beach. Our procedure was for one person to stay in the boat off shore while the other two people were dropped off at different places on shore. The beach walkers each carried a rifle in case we came upon any bears. One beach walker and the person in the boat each had a walkie-talkie.

As I was walking my stretch of beach, which was quite rocky, I came upon a wide stream. As I slowly picked my way across, the rushing water was up to the top of my hip boots. The rocks on the bottom were slick with moss and I lost my footing and fell into the freezing water. Completely drenched, I had to wait over a half hour for the boat to pick me up. Fortunately, this was a rare, sunny day.

After I warmed up we decided to walk beach on the other side of Sheep Bay. This time I stayed in the boat so I could dry off my clothes. I dropped Turk off at one spot at 4:30 PM and was going to drop Sheridan off further along the same side of the beach to walk in the same direction. The plan was for Turk to stop hiking at the spot where Sheridan was left off on the beach. However, we didn't decide exactly where that spot would be when we dropped Turk off. As Turk was climbing out of the boat he suggested that I drop Sheridan off up the coast about halfway to Sheep Point, the end of Sheep Bay. Then I should hover around the drop-off spot in the boat, and Turk would hike to there.

As I was driving Sheridan to his drop-off site, we agreed that it made more sense to drop him off at Sheep Point, so he could walk toward Turk, and they would meet somewhere in the middle. As they walked the beach I took the boat to the middle of the bay, stripped, and hung my clothes to dry in the sun. After two hours of watching and counting otters through the binoculars, I drove along the beach to find Sheridan and Turk. I spotted Sheridan, but not Turk. Sheridan had walked way past the expected meeting point, almost to where we had dropped off Turk, but he never met Turk. Sheridan got in the boat and we cruised slowly along the shoreline looking for Turk, but it became obvious that he was not standing on the beach waiting to be picked up. Something had gone awry. We decided that the best plan would be to go back to the point where we left Turk on the beach, anchor the boat, and retrace his path on foot.

The shoreline of Sheep Bay, like much of Prince William Sound, is not a flat beach. There are sections that vary from gravel to basketball-sized rocks, to small boulders, intermixed with high, steep, jagged cliffs, which abut the forest. At each cliff, we climbed to the top and one of us walked along the outside edge while the other one walked parallel, further into the forest, as we called for Turk. This was a very slow process and after three hours we realized there wasn't enough daylight left in the day to search all of the cliffs. I began to panic and could only imagine the worst possible scenario. The cliffs were precarious with moss-covered, jagged, crumbly rocks and deep fissures. It was very apparent that someone traversing along the edge in rubber boots could easily slip and fall and crack their skull on the rocks below. We decided that we needed help. As a last ditch effort, Sheridan fired several shots with the rifle into the air, hoping Turk would do the same. I heard a noise and said to Sheridan, "That's him!" but Sheridan said it was just an echo. We decided that I would take the boat to Cordova to get help and Sheridan would remain on the beach.

Before I left for Cordova, Sheridan insisted that we write down all of the information to show potential rescuers in town. He thought I was too panicked and might misconstrue the details. I was furious because I knew where I was and knew what had happened. I did not want to waste any more time before getting help. I left Sheridan on the beach and sped toward Cordova. I thought I heard another shot so I slowed down and heard Sheridan yelling at me so I roared away in disgust. I stopped at a fishing boat on the way to town to use their radio to call the Coast Guard. Their radio did not reach the Coast Guard so we tried to call a boat in Nelson Bay and have them call the Coast Guard. The other boat could not reach the Coast Guard, either. When I reached Cordova, I stopped at a fishing boat in the harbor and used their radio to call the Coast Guard, who, in turn, told me to go to the state trooper's office. The fisherman had his truck at the harbor parking lot and kindly gave me a ride to the state trooper's office. After five minutes, our friend, Dick Groff, burst into the office and said he had four Forest Service boats and fifteen people forty-five minutes away from Sheep Bay who could help us search for Turk. His secretary had heard my call to the Coast Guard on her scanner and immediately called Dick at home.

Suddenly, the phone rang in the state trooper's office. When the trooper hung up he calmly said that Turk was found, he was fine, and that he and Sheridan were waiting for me to pick them up. I said in disbelief, "There's no way! How could anyone know that? Who was that on the phone?" The trooper told me that the call was from the Coast Guard but he did not know how they found out. I felt somewhat relieved, but worried that I did not have the full story. Dick, knowing that I was still frazzled, insisted that he come with me to Sheep Bay to pick them up, even though it was late.

We traveled in the dark and when we arrived in Sheep Bay we saw a bright light on the beach. As we got closer to shore we saw a fire on land and two dark bodies standing nearby. I drove the boat up to shore, leaped out, and hugged Turk.

I soon learned that shortly after I left for Cordova, Sheridan had found Turk on the beach. Sheridan heard Turk's gunshot as I was speeding away. He looked down the beach and saw Turk waving his t-shirt. Once they were together, they figured that they must have passed each other on a cliff without knowing it. One of them went along the top of the cliff and the other apparently walked below on the narrow shelf of rock at the water's edge. Turk got all the way to Sheep Point and then started to walk back. While he was walking, he never knew exactly where he was or where the supposed meeting spot might be. He did not know that Sheridan was walking toward him. He did not realize how far he had gone until he arrived at Sheep Point, when he could see around the bend, beyond Sheep Bay. Not having a walkie-talkie, he had no way to communicate with Sheridan, or me, so he just started walking back. At one point he heard Sheridan's rifle shots, and shot back. The "echo" that we heard was not an echo at all. It was Turk answering us. Also, Turk saw me drive the boat away, fired his last shot, and yelled to me. I had slowed the boat down, but because I thought it was Sheridan's voice, I continued on my way, too harried to look back.

When Sheridan met up with Turk, they decided to try to reach someone using the walkie-talkie. Previously, we only used the walkie-talkies to talk to each other, and we knew the range was short. They tried all four channels, and remarkably reached the Coast Guard via a repeating station in the mountains, and the Coast Guard, in turn, called the state trooper in Cordova to give him the message.

We got back to camp at 1:30 AM, famished and exhausted from all the stress. We cooked a big pot of spaghetti and recounted the events and lessons of the day. Foremost, we learned to never change plans mid-stream. Our problems that day stemmed from the fact that Sheridan and I changed plans after Turk was dropped off on the beach. Because Turk didn't have a walkie-talkie, we couldn't inform him of our revised, seemingly better, plan. Second, we learned that in case of future emergencies, we could reach the Coast Guard on our walkie-talkie, at least from some places. We would again find that necessary in the months to come. Finally, we reflected on all the Alaskans who generously offered their help.

In this unforgiving environment they watch out for each other as a means of survival. Although we were outsiders—university students living in a tent camp well out of town—we had been treated as part of the local community. Nobody ridiculed us for being dumb or green. In fact, the local fishermen on the dock, the guys at the Forest Service and at the outboard motor shop, and those we met in the grocery store when we came to town, were all fascinated by our research. They marveled at us living in a tent in the perpetual rain and scooting about in our small, open, skiffs. "Everybody makes mistakes," they said. "And the important thing is to be more careful next time because you may not get the chance to learn the same lesson twice." These Alaskans, unkempt in their rubber boots and rain gear, often smelling of fish and cigarettes, were the kindest, most caring people that I had ever met. I went to sleep that night comforted by that thought, not knowing how many more times they would come to our rescue.

# Bears At Camp

We slept soundly until 10:30 AM and then went to Cordova to pick up the starter from the outboard motor shop. We took advantage of being in town, and took showers, did laundry, bought food, and did other errands. We wondered how many people in town heard my call for help on the scanner, like Dick's secretary.

The next day Turk and I each drove a boat into Nelson Bay to radiotrack. Sheridan stayed at camp and listened to radio-signals at the automatic tracking station to see if the receiver was capturing the signals. While I was radiotracking, I saw a raft of fifty otters. I turned off the motor and drifted toward the raft as it broke up into two smaller rafts. As the boat got closer to them, I identified five of "our" otters by the colors of their tags and transmitters. When I got closer, I noticed how social the otters were acting. Two small otters were rolling and touching each other with their front paws. Other otters were grooming themselves, touching a neighboring otter's head with a front paw, diving together, or playing "piggyback" with another otter. Sometimes three or four otters were interacting with each other. Then some otters became very curious about the boat and approached me, circled the boat, dove, periscoped, and dove again, or sculled away on their backs. Otters normally swim on their backs—in this position they could keep a close eye on me. If they thought I was too close to them, they quickly dove and swam away underwater.

It was interesting to see how the otters used their small front paws like hands. They scratched themselves vigorously or gently rubbed their heads or cheeks. Sometimes they would lightly tap a nearby otter. Most amazing, was the way they could manipulate food items. They could quickly pop a series of small items into their mouth, or using both their paws and teeth, crack open large clams. To ingest large crabs, they would pull off each individual leg and eat it before tackling the body.

Later that day we examined the first roll of strip chart paper from the tracking station and were mystified to find that signals for most of the otters had not recorded at night. We wondered if the otters left Nelson Bay at night, or if they used parts of the bay that were beyond the range of the tracking station. We tested this by taking a transmitter far out into the bay to see if the automatic station would record the signal. It picked up the signal throughout the whole bay. That still left the possibility that otters vacated the bay at night. We also considered an alternate theory. Maybe the otters were so active at night that the tracking station could not pick up their signals because they were frequently underwater searching for food. This seemed doubtful, though, that each otter would be underwater every time the receiver scanned its frequency. And furthermore, why did this only happen at night? Could the signal reception be diminished at night due to some atmospheric effect? None of these explanations seemed satisfactory. Our first scientific challenge was to explain this phenomenon.

The next day provided more insight into this puzzle. At 5:30 PM we were radiotracking and could not locate several otters. Suddenly, one hour later, a few of them reappeared not far from where we had been radiotracking. We saw several of them grooming, which, from the little data we had, suggested that they had just finished feeding. But that still did not explain why we could not receive their signals when they were eating on the surface of the water. This perplexing quandary was bothersome to both of us.

That night Turk and I looked again at the data from the automatic tracking station. We found that otters were consistently "gone" from 1:00 AM–5:00 AM and they were consistently present from 8:00 AM–3:00 PM and, again, from 8:00 PM–1:00 AM. Turk decided that he would radiotrack all night in Nelson Bay to see if otters left the bay. Sheridan and I stayed at camp.

At 10:00 PM I went to the "bathroom"—a toilet seat that straddled across two logs over a deep pit, 150 feet from the tent. It was an outhouse without the house. The thick alder brush provided natural walls. As I was walking to the site, I stepped over a log thirty feet from the tent, and just missed stepping on a large, fresh bear scat. I had gone to the bathroom three hours earlier and the scat was not there. I ran back to the tent and told Sheridan. We each grabbed a rifle and searched around the tent area. We did not find any other signs of bears. However, we were quite nervous so we each decided to sleep with a rifle beside our sleeping bag. We knew that both black bears and brown bears lived in this area, and we were hoping that the scat was from a less aggressive black bear. It took forever to get to sleep. I grabbed the rifle whenever I heard a noise. We were fortunate to not have any bears visit the camp that night. That would happen later.

Turk got back to camp at 7:00 AM and commented how tired he was from staying up all night. I was also exhausted but it was my shift to radiotrack. By a twist of good luck, the bay was so fogged in I could not go out in the boat and was able to sleep until noon. Before we fell asleep Turk quipped, "The mystery continues—all the otters were in the bay close to camp throughout the night." I said, "That's nice, so were the bears!"

In the late afternoon we all went out to untangle the capture net. This was a tedious job and Turk never had much patience for it. The only open area to do this was on the rocky beach. When it was low tide in the late afternoon the mosquitoes and gnats were especially thick on the beach. They flew into our noses and mouths, adding enormously to the frustration of picking the net. The insect repellent seemed to do nothing. Turk got so grouchy I sent him back to bed.

After dinner, Turk announced that he would track all night again and get to the bottom of the missing otter mystery. When he returned the next morning, he had discovered that the otters were feeding most of the night and did not leave Nelson Bay. We looked at the automatic tracking station recorder and none of the otters were marked on the paper! Although we had taken a step closer to solving the mystery, the explanation for the missing data was still beyond our reach. Eventually solving this enigma would be exciting, but even having to figure it out was exhilarating. I found myself determined to find the answer. I never knew at the outset of this project that there would be so many mysteries to solve and how difficult it was to test competing hypotheses. This was far from a controlled laboratory situation.

When Turk slept the next morning, I radiotracked in Nelson Bay. I saw 143 otters. As I was identifying individuals through the binoculars, I heard a blowing noise in the water. I looked up and a porpoise swam ten feet from the boat. It surfaced and dove three times. I was so amazed at all the creatures living below the surface.

That afternoon, we all went to the Reluctant Fisherman, a hotel and restaurant in Cordova, to pick up Don from the University of Minnesota. He brought nineteen more transmitters with him and came up to see how we were doing on the study. He asked us how the fishing was, and we had to admit that we did not have time to check it out because the study was all-consuming.

Each radio-transmitter was shaped like a cylinder, was two and one-half inches long, three-quarters of an inch in diameter, and had a twelve-inch whip antenna. The transmitter was attached to the hind flipper of an otter using two small bolts, one on either side of the middle digit. There was a small foam pad on both sides of the flipper, in an attempt to make the transmitter as comfortable as possible.

The previous winter Turk had tested the rate of corrosion of different kinds of metal in salt-water aquariums. The best design, he found, was for the bolts to be a different type of metal than the nuts. The idea was for the nuts to corrode and, thereby, release the transmitter in about a year. Despite this controlled, elegant, laboratory experiment, we would later find that it did not quite work exactly this way in the field.

After painting the transmitters all different colors, we got Don to help us untangle the last net on the beach. It took hours. Oddly enough, Don seemed to like this monotonous task. Perhaps it was a nice break from the office work at the university. After untangling the net, we only put one net in the water because we were concerned about catching too many otters at once.

Turk got up at 4:00 AM to do the first net check of the day, but he could not find the net! He came back to camp and woke us up. We put on our several layers of warm clothes and rain gear and went out in the boat looking for the net. We searched half an hour and found it further out in Nelson Bay. The anchor had dragged and the net drifted.

Sheridan checked the net again at noon and saw twenty-seven otters rafting nearby. He felt certain that they would float into the net. We loaded the equipment in the boat and went out to the net, but no otters were caught and the raft had dispersed. Had the day with the thirteen otters made us more nervous, or just over-confident?

With four of us at camp, the main tent was a bit crowded. We brought another tent with us from Minnesota for this occasion. However, last week in anticipation of Don's arrival, when we went to set it up, we discovered that the poles were missing. Sheridan informed us that his roommate had taken the poles from Turk's office several months earlier and forgot to return them. That roommate, who worked at United Parcel Service (UPS), promised to ship the poles last week. We went to Cordova and asked for the UPS office but we were told that there was none. We called Sheridan's roommate and he told us that he saved shipping costs by sneaking the box of poles into a stack of outgoing packages, not knowing that UPS did not (then) deliver to Alaska. Hence, instead of paying shipping charges, we had to buy a small tent in town.

We decided to stop and talk to Dick Groff at the Forest Service and update him on our study. We told him that Ancel would soon take one of the boats that we were using back to Anchorage. Dick said he could get us another boat if we needed it. Dick was always in a good mood and would do anything for us. He told us we were his "favorite people" and we viewed him as a father figure.

Back at camp that night as we ate dinner, a thundering sound startled us. We ran outside and saw a rockslide three hundred feet from camp. Large boulders were rolling down the side of the mountain. Looking around, there were recent signs of avalanches on all the nearby mountain slopes. We came to the realization that this environment was very much in flux. The alders around our camp were only four to five feet tall, indicating they were quite young. What sort of catastrophe occurred during the last decade to create this shelf of land that we were now camping on? We would learn the answer to that question the following year.

The next morning Turk and I were out in a boat and saw three rafts of otters near the net. We drove the boat fifty feet from a raft, turned off the motor, and allowed the boat to quietly drift toward the otters. We were hoping to chase some otters into the net. As the otters floated to within five feet of the net, they suddenly dove and came up on the far side. Apparently, they detected the net. However, one small dark-headed otter got caught. It was a small forty-three-pound male. After we drugged him, and during the time we were working him up, another otter kept swimming up to our boat and then swam up to the net and dove under it. It stayed near us for over an hour. Could it have been the mother of the captured otter? The small otter was certainly older than a pup so the behavior of this larger otter seemed very unusual.

Although there seemed to be some affiliation between these two otters, Turk decided to take the captured otter to Sheep Bay and release him there. Turk and I planned to track the otter all night. For this occasion we had previously designed a "boat bed." We had found some tongue-and-groove boards on the beach and cut them to the width of the boat. When hooked together, and set across the gunnels, a person could sleep in a sleeping bag on the small platform. Since it was pouring rain, we also picked up a tarp that we could erect over the bed.

After releasing the otter in Sheep Bay, we put together the boat bed and set up the tarp. For dinner, we cooked some hot dogs over a propane torch. Later that night, I was the first to try out the boat bed. Cozy in my sleeping bag under the tarp, after being rocked to sleep by the slow undulations of the boat, Turk suddenly hit the gas because our otter was on the move. The boat tilted up and I rolled out the back of the boat bed into several inches of water on the floor by the motor. Lying in my soaking wet sleeping bag I thought, "Oh great! Another first!"

At 3:00 AM the radio-transmitter quit sending a signal. This transmitter had a delay mode so it worked for twelve hours and then went off for twelve hours in order to save battery life. Needless to say, I was quite happy when this occurred so we could take the boat back to camp, a fifty-minute ride, and dry off. When we pulled up to the boat mooring we were surprised to see Don standing on the beach. When he heard the motor approaching he jumped into his rain gear. He said he was worried about us and couldn't sleep well. He kept picturing "that screwy boat bed and someone rolling out the back of the boat." I told him that it nearly happened and we would need to make some modifications before it could be used again.

Back in the tent we decided to have a hot breakfast of oatmeal and toast. Making toast on a Coleman stove was quite an art, and we never fully perfected it. We had purchased a handheld grate specifically for making toast over an open flame. It had to be watched like a hawk. One minute it would be warm bread, and the next it was charred black and smoking.

Over breakfast we decided to increase our net checks to four times a day to reduce the chance of catching several fighting otters. Nevertheless, at the 3:00 PM check, we had ten otters in the net. Luckily, none of the otters were caught in the same spot so there were no fights. We used both boats to work up the otters, Turk and I in one and Sheridan and Don in the other.

The veterinarian that had given us the drugs had sent Don a new drug to test on the otters. This drug, Wydase, increases the absorption rate of the fentanyl and azaparone so it should take less time to anesthetize the otters. We didn't understand the need for this drug because most otters were anesthetized in six minutes. However, we used it at various dosages to satisfy the wishes of the veterinarian, who provided these expensive drugs to us for free. After all, everything we were doing was part of a scientific investigation. The two otters that received the highest dose had convulsions. Fortunately, the seizures did not last long and the otters recovered quickly. Although the otters were anesthetized more quickly, we saw more risk than benefit when using this drug.

Surprisingly, one of the ten otters was a female. By now we had recognized that Nelson Bay was a male area. Previous researchers had discovered that several populations of sea otters exhibited sexual segregation—females and a few breeding males occupied the core of the range, whereas concentrations of males lived at the expanding fronts of the range. Nelson Bay was at the edge of this expanding Prince William Sound population. We wondered how this rare female, whom we named "Kate," would get along with all these males.

After we worked up one male otter and released him, he kept swimming up to other otters in the net. He would bite their noses, grab their necks with his forepaws, and dive close to them. It seemed as if he were trying to help other otters get out of the net. Another otter did the same thing after he was released. In so doing, he was recaptured, and we had to disentangle him from the net.

These behaviors were curious and interesting. We saw the same thing again on other occasions. This also added context to our previous observation of the "mothering" behavior of the large otter toward the one that we had just taken to Sheep Bay. It now seemed more likely that the larger otter was also a male. For some reason, these males exhibited a form of altruism toward one another. At this point we could barely speculate why this was so. However, it seemed to go along with their rafting behavior and their frequent interactions within these rafts. Whether they knew each other as individuals was not clear (although we suspect they did), but obviously they were quite social, at least in this high-density area. Later, we would find that their sociality was more muted in a lower density, female-dominated area.

Turk wanted to take some of these otters even further away, to test the limits of their knowledge of this part of the sound. We chose a release site in St. Matthew's Bay (fig. 1) in Port Gravina, which was another hour (by boat) past Sheep Bay. We picked up the gear for the boat bed because this was going to be an all night affair. Unfortunately, we hadn't had any time to make modifications to it. As we were transporting four drugged otters in two boats, we saw a sea lion in the water. It was a very large, sleek, dark brown animal that swam with its face and whiskers out of the water.

Turk and I stayed with the otters in St. Matthew's Bay while Don and Sheridan went back to camp. We spent another night in the famous boat bed but this time we learned to accelerate the boat more slowly if one of us was sleeping.

We were now one week from the summer solstice, where the sun does not set above the Arctic Circle. Here, in Prince William Sound (60–61°N latitude), it was only dark from 11:30 PM–1:00 AM so we could see quite well for most of the night. All four transmittered otters stayed in St. Matthew's Bay. We tracked them until 3:00 PM the next day and then drove back to camp, exhausted. It had rained on and off the whole time we were in the boat.

We decided that we had captured enough otters and took the net out of the water. As we pulled the net up on the beach in a tarp, there was a salmon caught in it and we saved it for dinner. What a nice surprise!

The next day we drove back to Port Gravina to walk the beach all day and look for sea otter feces and bones. We hoped that the lessons learned from our mishap in Sheep Bay would prevent another calamity. As we were heading toward Port Gravina, a minke whale jumped fifteen feet out of the water, only one hundred feet in front of us. It repeated this show three times! Minke whales are the smallest baleen whales, are twenty-five to thirty feet long, and have two blowholes. They are very dark gray on the top of their body, lighter gray on the underside, and have a white band on each flipper. I was ready to take a picture if the whale breached again, but it didn't.

While we were in Port Gravina we saw nine female sea otters with pups. Obviously this was a female otter area. We wondered whether our four transplanted males might like it here. However, when we took the boat into St. Matthew's Bay, we found that only two of them were still there.

As we were driving back to camp the water got really rough near Point Gravina again. I had a flashback of the time Turk and I were here in an overloaded boat and waves were breaking over the bow. My heart started to pound. This time we were not overloaded with gear, so the waves did not come in over the bow, and I started to relax. It was a long, slow, bumpy boat ride but we made it back to camp without any problems. As usual, it rained most of the day and pelted our faces the whole way back. We often thought it would have been nice to have a windshield on the boat.

The following day we located the missing two otters from St. Matthew's Bay. They had come back to Nelson Bay—a distance of twenty miles! We realized that the otters knew their way around a large part of Prince William Sound and they had preferences on where they wanted to be. Apparently, a group of females did not entice the males to stay. We presumed there must have been a good reason for coming back.

That afternoon, we went to Cordova to pick up another professor, Peter, from the University of Minnesota. He was a colleague of Don's and was coming up to study hermit crabs and stay at our camp. Our camp was now getting a little crowded, although our conversations became quite diverse.

When we radiotracked the following day, a third otter that we had taken to St. Matthew's Bay was back in Nelson Bay. As we were radiotracking we saw porpoises. They swam fifty feet from us and frequently surfaced on each side of the boat after taking shallow dives, and appeared to be chasing us. It suddenly occurred to me that every day in Prince William Sound was totally different. One can see more wildlife in a day here than most people see in their lifetime.

We pulled the boat up to a small rock outcrop called Hank's Island, because we were curious about all the terns flying overhead. As we approached the rocks the terns started squawking loudly. When we climbed up on the rocks we could see why they were so upset. There were tern nests with mottled eggs everywhere we looked, just a few feet from each other, and some of the eggs were hatching. We felt guilty about disturbing their colony and quickly departed.

Sheridan left the next day to go back to Minneapolis. Turk and I radiotracked in the afternoon and discovered that the otter that we had taken to Sheep Bay several days before was back in Nelson Bay. Don and Peter took the second boat to radiotrack and fish. Don promised that we would have fresh fish for dinner. I had visions of having a wonderful fish fry—but, as fishermen are always boastful, we ended up eating spaghetti.

We brought Don to Cordova a few days later because he was going back to Minnesota. When we were in town we met a fisherman, named Craig, who also studied whales. He told us that some fishermen were asking him what was going on with the sea otters because some of them had wires in their feet! He also told us that the crab fishermen were really angry at the sea otters because they were eating a lot of Dunguness crabs.

The following day we decided to radiotrack in Orca Inlet (fig. 1) while Peter stayed at camp. The water was very shallow in the inlet. The boat suddenly came to a halt when we came aground on a mud bar, and Turk and I lunged forward. After we pulled ourselves off the floor of the boat, we jumped in the water with our hip boots and had to push hard to dislodge the boat. Luckily, the prop was not damaged.

When we got back to camp, Peter came running out to us and said he heard a loud noise when he was in the tent. He opened the tent flap and saw the Weber grill lying on its side on the ground. A few yards from the grill was an adult black bear that, Peter estimated, weighed 250 pounds. Peter did not have a rifle because we had taken them with us. He stared into the eyes of the bear and it turned around and slowly walked away, but did not appear to be scared. He would be back! Peter was happy to be leaving the next day.

The next morning we brought Peter to Cordova and stopped by to see Dick Groff. We brought him a long overdue bottle of wine. He told us he quit his job at the Forest Service and his last day would be in two weeks. He was concerned that his replacement might not let us keep our trailer in the Forest Service compound. Therefore, he wrote a contract that we all signed allowing us to keep it there until the end of the study. Later, Dick's prediction came true and we used the contract to keep the trailer in place. In our conversation, we also told Dick that we were coming back to Cordova the next night to go out to eat and dance because it was our third wedding anniversary. Dick not only told us a great place to go, but he said we could borrow his truck to get there!

The next morning we cleaned the boats and reorganized our camp. This was our first day since the start of our study with just the two of us. Our gas supply at camp was getting low so we pumped the last gas out of the fifty-five-gallon storage drums into six-gallon cans that we used to run the boats. We then placed the two empty fifty-five-gallon drums into the boat to bring to Cordova. In Cordova, we filled the drums at the marine gas dock. This was quite a challenge, especially on a low, incoming tide. The tidal force would push our small boat under the gas dock. One of us had to maneuver the boat while the other grabbed one of the pilings—no simple feat, as the three-foot diameter pilings were covered with slippery algae and sharp barnacles. Once we were tied up to a piling the gas hose was lowered thirty feet to reach us so we could fill the drums as the boat bounced up and down in the waves. Later, we would have to get the 450-pound drums out of the boat and onto the beach. To do this, we would dump the drums over the side of the boat into the shallow water and roll them up the rocky beach to a point above the high tide mark.

Before heading back to camp and dealing with the gas drums, we went into town for our big date. We met up with Dick, borrowed his truck, and drove six miles out of town to a restaurant called the Black Sheep. We had a great meal and danced to a fun, live band. Our anniversary gifts to each other were "Alaska clothes"—thermal underwear and wool socks. A final luxury for our anniversary—we stayed in our trailer that night.

The next day we met Ancel Johnson in Cordova. He had just flown in from Green Island, in central Prince William Sound, on a small floatplane and planned to meet his wife in town and take one of the boats that we had been using to Olsen Bay. Ancel had built a small cabin on Green Island so he could study sea otters there, and he was going to let us use it for our study. Looking back, we realize how uncommonly generous Ancel was to us. Instead of protecting his turf as the only Alaskan sea otter biologist, he opened his arms to us. He shared his equipment, research site, and most of all, his wealth of knowledge and ideas about sea otters. He recognized the value of the new radio-telemetry work that we were embarking on as well as other components of our study. He also valued (and maybe was a little jealous of) the extended time that we could spend in the field. We talked to Ancel about sea otter biology and study logistics for over four hours.

We planned to use Green Island as a second study site because it was a female otter area. Unlike Nelson Bay, which was newly occupied by otters this year, otters had been living at Green Island for at least thirty years. Ancel informed us of several key contacts for maintaining our field camp at Green Island. Green Island is more than sixty miles from Cordova and it would not be feasible to drive three hours one-way to Cordova every week to buy groceries and supplies. Ancel told us that the Alaska Department of Fish and Game had a large boat, the *Montague,* and the Department of Transportation had a boat, the *Enforcer,* that could possibly haul fifty-five-gallon drums of gas to us. He also mentioned that a local small air charter company, called Chitina Air, did regular mail runs to the outer reaches of Prince William Sound and might, for a small fee, deliver groceries and mail to us. This proved to be vital information.

The next day at camp we spent several hours repairing the otter net. Sometimes when an otter was extremely tangled we had to cut the net to get it out. Before returning Ancel's net, we had to mend all the cut lines.

Later in the day, we started a second major component of our study—feeding observations. We had a spotting scope and also a high-powered Questar telescope that Ancel let us use for our study. If an otter was feeding within two hundred yards off shore we could use the telescope to identify the type of food it was eating. One of us would record data while the other person observed through the telescope. The observer would say "up" when the otter came up to the surface, and "down" when the otter dove again. The recorder used a specialized stopwatch that recorded "lap times" (found on many wristwatches today, but unusual in those days) to clock the otter's surface times and submerged times. When the otter was on the surface, the observer also called out what the otter was eating and how many items were eaten. We also judged the size of the items in relation to the width of the otter's paw. We realized how fortunate we were to be studying a species in which you could see every food item that was eaten. We recorded data for one and one-half hours on one otter and a half hour on another one. The dive times and surface times were remarkably consistent. It was fun collecting this data and it was a nice change from trapping and radiotracking.

Most amazingly, this first day of foraging observations provided the answer to the mystery of the missing nighttime data at the automatic tracking station. The second otter that we observed happened to be one that we had transmittered. We noticed that when the otter was on the surface consuming food, its hind flippers were usually horizontal. The transmitter and the whip antenna were, thus, a few inches underwater. This is quite different from the normal resting position when the flippers are vertical and the antenna stands straight out of the water. Realizing that this was an important finding, we grabbed the receiver and a handheld antenna and listened to the signal. Sure enough, the signal was very weak and difficult to hear even though the otter was on the surface. That means that the tracking station would not pick up the signal from a feeding otter if it was not close by. This explained why there was no data recorded during the night when the otters were feeding. It was a thrill to have solved the puzzle!

When we returned to camp we saw a harbor seal splashing around in the water. This seal had been splashing in the water for many nights in a row. As we walked up to one of our coolers in the stream to get some food for dinner, we saw that the cover was off and lying on the ground. It had two holes in it that looked like holes from bear teeth. I guess our bear friend was back at camp.

The next afternoon, after radiotracking, we noticed that a bear had bitten into a case of two-cycle oil that was sitting on the rocky beach beside the fifty-five-gallon drums of gas. It bit through a box and into one quart of oil. Oil was leaking all over the ground. After cleaning it up, I walked up a hill to the automatic tracking station and there was a big bear scat on the first step. We became very nervous about the possibility of a bear coming into our tent. It was time for more target practice!

Despite the bears, each day our camp was becoming more and more beautiful. Wildflowers were in bloom everywhere. We saw columbines, lupine, wild geraniums, and bluebells. It was a very romantic setting, and it was nice that Turk and I were alone at camp.

The following day we planned to take some supplies, including the nets, back to the Olsen Bay warehouse and then spend the night with Ancel and his wife, Barb, at the dilapidated cabins in the back of Olsen Bay. We walked down the beach toward the nets and immediately recognized that something was wrong. We had left each net in a neat, folded pile on a tarp, but now they were strewn about. When we got closer, we saw they were all tangled again. Our mischievous bear friend had been at work.

Eventually, we untangled and restacked the nets and loaded them into the boat. The nets were heavy and the boat was overloaded (again) as we headed for Olsen Bay. I was nervous that we would hit rough waters at Point Gravina. The water in Nelson Bay was rough but we were fortunate that it calmed down as we traveled west.

After returning the supplies to the warehouse, we hiked back to the Olsen Bay cabins. The half-mile windy path followed a long narrow stream and was bordered by grass as tall as me. Barb and Ancel were waiting for us. They fed us homemade clam chowder and rockfish fillets, fresh from Olsen Bay. We had a wonderful evening talking and drinking wine. Ancel mentioned that he had seen a number of brown bears by the stream that we walked by to get to the cabins. As the night went on, we found ourselves talking to each other in the pitch dark. The darkness was broken only by the red glow of Ancel's pipe each time he inhaled. Ancel was averse to artificial light in a field camp setting so he did not want to light the gas lantern. It seemed, in the darkness, that the spoken words had even more meaning.

The next morning Barb showed me how she fed a Steller's jay named "Blue." She placed pieces of pancakes on the roof of one of the cabins. Blue came and ate the pancakes, and then ate some pieces out of my hand.

Turk and I left at 9:00 AM and radiotracked in all the bays on the way back to camp. Ancel and Barb later came to camp and joined us for lunch and more "shop talk."

Over the next several days we radiotracked and located most of the otters. We also spent many hours at the automatic tracking station. One of us watched how it recorded on the paper while the other one looked through the telescope at the activities of nearby transmittered otters. As a result, we became confident in how to interpret the data on the paper and, thus, were able to determine how much time individual otters were resting or feeding each day.

We also spent a lot of time collecting more feeding observations. Otters were very consistent in their dive times and surface times when they were feeding in the same depth of water on the same food items. If they came up empty handed they would quickly catch their breath and dive back down within ten seconds. It was interesting and entertaining to watch them eat. An otter would take a couple bites and then roll over in the water and return to its back. It appeared like it was washing scraps off its chest when it rolled over.

We hadn't been to Cordova for over a week so we did not have the opportunity to take showers—we did not have modern facilities at camp. Therefore, we decided to utilize a "make-shift" sauna that Sheridan had built. It was in the shape of an igloo, made out of bent branches and covered in heavy plastic. We made a fire inside, heated up some rocks, and after pouring water over the rocks it became very hot and steamy. It felt great, however, we could not make it an authentic sauna and take the plunge into the cold stream because it was far too frigid.

On the fourth of July we went to Cordova to attend Dick Groff's going away party. We met the families of the people who worked at the Forest Service and also met Dick's replacement district ranger, Fred. He was presently living in a trailer at the Forest Service warehouse, but his family did not accompany him.

The next morning, we chartered a flight with Chitina Air to radiotrack and count the otters in northeast Prince William Sound. When we arrived at Chitina Air, the pilot was not there. The owner went to the back room and called him on the phone. All we heard was, "Frank, where are you? Are you too hung-over to fly?" I thought to myself, "We are dead for sure!" Fifteen minutes later, a twenty-five-year-old "kid" (like us!) came in the door wearing a ripped t-shirt and jeans with his hair sticking out all over his head. He looked like he had just jumped out of bed. We walked with him over to the pond where the four-passenger floatplane was tied up and I hopped into the back seat. Turk attached an antenna to each of the wings and ran a cable from the antennas to the receiver. He held the receiver in his lap and wore headphones so he could hear the radio-signals of the otters when we flew over them. For the next two hours we flew over several bays and circled, many times, over every group of otters, so we could count them. The pilot informed me that I was the first back seat passenger that did not get sick!

Suddenly, the pilot yelled out, "Ow!" as he grabbed his left cheek with his hand. The plane swerved to the right. We were only two hundred feet above the water. I had no idea what was happening. I only knew that we did not know how to fly the floatplane. The pilot told us he had a bad toothache. However, he continued to fly another hour until we were finished with the survey. We felt quite relieved when we landed back in the pond at Chitina Air. We were also extremely happy that we found three of seven missing otters in a bay near Orca Inlet. It was low tide when we flew over this bay, and there were approximately one hundred otters hauled out on the mud. We had never seen this before. After our flight we conducted errands in Cordova, took the boat back to camp, and figured that sometime we should take the boat to Orca Inlet in low tide to observe the hauled-out otters.

The next morning we got up very early to watch the process by which the otters congregated in rafts in Nelson Bay. We had noticed that otters rested in big rafts during the late morning, but hadn't previously documented how these rafts formed. At 5:00 AM all the otters that we saw were feeding. At 7:30 AM, two otters were resting near each other. Twenty minutes later, a big white-headed otter joined them, followed by four other otters. Then otters swam in from all directions, some of them still finishing their breakfast as they paddled on their backs toward the group. The water was flat calm and the ripples formed by swimming otters radiated out like the rays of the sun as they converged toward the group. By 8:00 AM there were thirty otters and by 8:30 AM there were one hundred otters resting together. We wondered how they knew the time and place of the morning raft formation. Could any otter be the seed for the large raft?

We noticed several things about raft formation. When otters joined the raft they seemed to look for particular individuals to interact with. In fact, they typically swam past several otters before finding the individuals that they were seeking. Sometimes if those individuals were not in that raft, they would leave and then find them in another nearby group. Upon finding their comrades, they would touch each other and "play wrestle" in the water while twisting and turning and doing somersaults. Some days the otters all got together in one large raft, whereas other days they formed several smaller rafts.

Over the next few days we continued to radiotrack the otters, collect feeding data, watch raft formation, and pack things up to bring back to the Olsen Bay warehouse and to bring to Green Island. There was another huge bear scat by the tracking station and a bear bit through the coffee can that held our toilet paper and carried the toilet paper sixty feet away from our "outhouse." By this time I was happy to be going to Green Island. The bears were getting a little too bold for comfort.

On July 10 we went to Cordova to arrange more logistics for Green Island. We went to the Department of Transportation and arranged for the captain of the *Enforcer* to bring out two fifty-five-gallon drums of gas to us. We then went to Chitina Air and arranged for them to stop at Green Island to deliver groceries every two weeks during their normal mail run. Next, we went to the grocery store and gave them a list of food items to deliver to Chitina Air in two weeks. We also arranged that we would send them grocery lists every two weeks after that. Upon the delivery of groceries to Green Island we would give the pilot a letter with the list to mail to the grocery store. The grocery store would do the shopping for us, deliver the items to Chitina Air, and bill us when we returned to town. This arrangement was formalized by a handshake—more Alaskan hospitality!

That evening we picked up Don and his daughter, Nancy, in town. They were going to Green Island with us. Nancy was only fourteen-years-old and had never been in the field with her dad.

The next day we packed the boat with more items to store at the Olsen Bay warehouse. The trip to Olsen Bay was uneventful because the water was fairly calm. However, on the way back to camp, we encountered our nemesis again in Port Gravina. The wind had picked up and the whitecaps were breaking toward us, but because the boat was empty, they did not break over the bow. As usual, though, it was pouring all day, and although we had heavy-duty rain gear, the pelting rain would work its way through the collar and wrists and soak our shirts. It had rained so much over the past month that the stream near our tent, which was a creek when we set up camp, was now a torrent. We had been here two months and I was excited about the impending change in scenery.

The next morning we packed up the rest of camp and all four of us went to Olsen Bay to store the items in the warehouse. We spent the night in the cabins. When we arrived at the cabins our friends, the Steller's jays, were still there and they ate food out of our hands. Although happy to leave our rain drenched tent camp, we had no idea what was in store for us at Green Island.

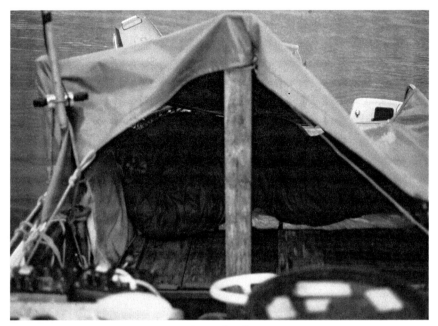

Boat bed

Observations through telescopes

# Green Island

On July 13 we walked along the long trail from the cabins in Olsen Bay to where the boat was moored in front of the warehouse. We heard some splashing in the stream and when we got to a spot where we were able to see through the tall grass, we saw a large brown bear catching salmon. The bear stood on its hind legs and sniffed in the air when he caught our scent. We walked very slowly and tried to get downwind of him. Feeling like we were a safe distance away, (although later wondering if that was true), we watched the bear for several minutes. There were so many salmon in the stream—he had no trouble catching them as he waded in the shallow water. After catching a fish in his mouth, he brought it to shore and quickly devoured it. Yesterday, when we walked along the stream, we noted that most of the salmon had only been partially eaten. The bear seemed to be selecting for the eggs of females and the brains of males.

When we arrived at the warehouse, we loaded the boat with the gear that we needed for Green Island. Standing back and looking at the boat, we realized that it was extremely overloaded. We also had a lot more gas than we normally carried, and four people instead of just the two of us. We were already somewhat nervous about this long trip and now even more so, recognizing that the boat was dangerously full. Nevertheless, we were committed to going. We decided we would assess how rough the water was in Port Gravina and then determine if we could make it to Green Island.

On the route to Green Island we would have to cross the Hinchinbrook Entrance (fig. 1), where Prince William Sound meets the open ocean. Therefore, if the water was rough in Port Gravina, it would be even worse in the ocean entrance. As we started out, we could not get the boat to plane on the water because the bow was so heavy. We rearranged the gear and Turk and Don sat on top of it. I drove the boat and it finally got up on the step (planed). Initially, it was choppy and foggy, but after a half hour the sun started to come out and the water became much calmer. We saw this as a good omen. Indeed, it stayed that way and two hours later we arrived at Green Island where the sun was shining brightly.

Green Island, named for the blanket of Sitka spruce trees that cover it, is quite a contrast to the two large islands, Montague and Knight, on either side of it. The two large islands have rocky, snowcapped mountains, whereas Green Island has low rolling hills. The seven-by-three-mile Green Island lies in a northeast-southwest direction. The northwest coast, where we were headed, had several small bays, inlets, and islands. Together these formed a safe harbor called Gibbon Anchorage (fig. 2). Fishermen frequently used Gibbon Anchorage to drop anchor for the night, especially in stormy weather. Otters were apparently attracted here as well, because it provided a safe place for females to raise pups. For this reason, Ancel chose to build his research cabin here.

We approached Gibbon Anchorage with excitement and a little trepidation. Ancel had warned us that there were lots of rocks, but did not say exactly where they were located. The last thing we wanted to do in the final leg of this journey was to ruin a prop, or worse yet, damage the lower end of the motor. It was nice to arrive at our destination, but we did not want to get stranded here. As we slowly entered the anchorage, I drove while Turk and Don laid on top of the heap of gear in the bow and looked in the water for submerged rocks. We maneuvered our way around various shallow spots and gravel bars and eventually rounded the turn into the arm that Ancel called "Camp Cove." Ahead of us was the cabin.

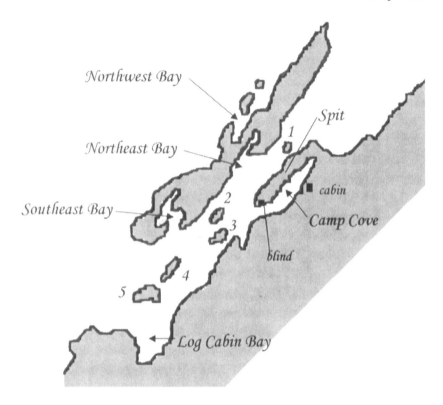

*Small islands – 1, 2, 3, 4, 5*

Figure 2. Gibbon Anchorage.

The entrance to the cabin was in the back. Inside, there was a three-foot-by-ten-foot entryway to hang up raincoats and store hip boots. Then an inside door led to the sleeping quarters. There were two built-in bunk beds on each side of the room. On the far side of the room another doorway led to the twelve-by-ten-foot kitchen and sitting area. On one side there was an oil stove. A Coleman stove sat on a narrow wooden stand along the back wall, which also had pots and pans on the lower shelf. There was a large window on each sidewall and another window on the front wall looking out into Camp Cove. The kitchen table was situated under that window. I pulled up a chair, sat down, and said, "I could live here." Don said,

"Look outside. You guys can do your research from right here in the cabin." Our overloaded boat was pulled up on the rocky beach and just behind it a white-headed otter was cruising on his back into Camp Cove, one flipper in the air, and one slowly paddling. Ancel told us about this otter and had named him "Crazy Otto." He was a male that resided in Camp Cove and was identifiable by a very specific nose scar.

We did a brief tour of the local area before the chore of unpacking the boat. The outside of the cabin had a long gutter along one side of the roof that angled down toward the back of the cabin. Below it, on the ground, there was a large metal bucket to collect rainwater. Fifty feet from the back door was a quaint little wooden outhouse. This meant there would be no more sitting on the toilet in the rain. Near the cabin there was a storage shed for gas drums, nets, and other gear, as well as a ten-foot rowboat. All around, the ground and trees were covered with moss and lichens, giving the area a very distinct, fresh, smell. The best thing about being on Green Island, however, was that there were no bears!

Although the cabin was much nicer than the tent in Nelson Bay, we did not sleep much the first night because of the mosquitoes. They buzzed our heads, and if my head stuck out of the sleeping bag, I got bitten. In fact, when I woke up my face was red from numerous bites.

After breakfast we drove the boat around the anchorage at low tide to map the location of all the various rocks that would be submerged at a higher tide. We also got out and explored the five small islands in the anchorage that Ancel had named "Islands One–Five," respectively, from north to south (fig. 2). We were looking for good sites from which to conduct observations. As we were driving around the anchorage, five porpoises kept surfacing around us, chasing and playing with each other. We also saw four female otters that had small, fuzzy pups on their chests. They would have given birth in May.

After our boat ride we went clamming. As we dug for clams, deer flies kept buzzing and landing on our heads, face, and hands. I was determined to make clam chowder for dinner so we kept digging until we collected thirty small littlenecks and soft-shelled clams.

The next day we set four capture nets in Gibbon Anchorage. Two days later we caught a forty-four-pound female and named her "Hazel." The workup went flawlessly and we felt we were off to a good start.

I was responsible for the net check that night at 10:00 PM. As I approached one net, I saw big brown eyes staring at me, surrounded by a large clump of net. I looked more closely and saw that we caught a harbor seal. It's head looked like a flattened egg and its body was like a smooth torpedo of blubber. It appeared to be very calm and was quite cute. I used a walkie-talkie to contact Turk and Don at the cabin and tell them the situation. Don told me to just "shake him out, it should be easy." As I approached the harbor seal he made loud grunts. I grabbed the net a short distance from him and he rolled and rolled getting more tangled, and grunted louder. He was obviously quite irritated. He also snapped his mouth open and closed and appeared eager to bite me. I realized there was no way I could get him out of the net, so I drove back to the cabin and picked up Turk and Don. When we returned to the net the three of us tried to "shake him out" but he kept rolling and getting even more tangled. Finally, Don pulled out a pocketknife and cut a huge hole in the net. The seal was finally free at 12:40 AM! Since it got dark at 11:30 PM we had to work in the dark for over an hour. Our standing joke for the rest of Don's stay, whenever we encountered a problem, was to say, "Just shake it out!"

The next night when we were driving the boat to check the nets, a sea otter was swimming very close to us. He was making a series of undulating shallow dives ("porpoising"), and coming up to breathe very quickly. Suddenly, we heard a thud on the side of the boat. We looked over and saw that we hit the otter! We stopped the boat, looked around nervously, and did not see him. Then he popped up about thirty yards away, looked back at us, and continued on his way, seemingly unfazed.

On July 18, the *Enforcer* arrived at Green Island. We drove the Boston Whaler out to the large boat and the captain used a winch to hoist two fifty-five-gallon drums of gas into our boat.

The captain invited us aboard and we had coffee with him and the crew. As we left the *Enforcer* the captain gave us a care package of ice cream and oranges. When we got to the beach in front of the cabin we had to push each fifty-five-gallon drum of gas into the water and roll it up the beach and into the shed. This was grueling work. However, the ice cream tasted great when we were finished. Since we had no refrigeration we had to eat it right away.

Later in the day, Turk and I went to set up an automatic tracking station on a ridge where one side faced Camp Cove and the other side had a precipice down to the beach. It was a ten-minute walk from the cabin. First, we had to pick out a tree that Turk could climb. We chose a one hundred and fifty-foot Sitka spruce at the edge of a two hundred-foot cliff, which would have a nice overview of Gibbon Anchorage and the surrounding area.

Turk tied a rope to his belt and began to climb. About three-quarters of the way up he stopped and I heard him talking to himself. There was a long pause and the rope that was dangling from his belt, and still partly coiled on the ground, did not move. I yelled up, "Are you okay?" He yelled back, "Hopefully. I wish I was taller." I couldn't see him through the branches but a few minutes later the dangling rope started moving upward again. Eventually, he called down to me to tie the two folded antennas and one end of the coaxial cable to the rope. After I did so, he hoisted the rope, removed the antennas, put them together, and U-bolted them to the tree. One pointed into Gibbon Anchorage, and the other faced the opposite direction. He then used a splitter to attach the coaxial cable to the antennas. After more than an hour in the tree, Turk was finally back on terra firma. "That was a scary climb," he said. "There was one place where I couldn't reach the next branch. I could clearly see down through the branches of the tree and down the cliff, all the way to the rocky beach. I kept wondering if it was worth trying to jump or if I should just come down and find another tree. I looked at the other trees around me, and none looked any better. It was only a one-foot vertical hop but my heart was pounding. I knew if I missed the grab for the upper branch I would be doomed. Coming down, as it turns out, was even harder because I had to hug the upper branch, then hang from it, freefall the one foot, and then quickly hug the trunk of the tree. I really hope I don't have to climb that sucker again!"

After Turk regained his composure, we connected the end of the coaxial cable to the receiver, and the receiver to the event recorder. We then programmed in Hazel's frequency, but heard nothing. To this day, Turk vividly remembers climbing that tree. However, his field notes recount the story this way—"Set up tracking station. It wasn't working too good, it didn't even record otter 801."

The site of this tracking station was quite scenic. All the trees were large and majestic, with dangling Spanish moss. Sitting near the edge of the cliff we had a great view of the anchorage and, in the other direction, the open expanse of Prince William Sound. The downside of this spot was that it seemed to be a haven for mosquitoes. I got bitten many times and thought that forcing someone to camp here for a night without a tent would be a great torture.

Afterward, we explored some of the terrain near the tracking station. We found a network of underground tunnels and holes in the moss that were river otter den sites. There was a strong stench in this area because the river otters had marked their territories with urine. There was also a lot of scat (spraint) from the river otters on the ground.

Every night so far on Green Island we had beautiful sunsets. From the beach in front of the cabin we could see the jagged peaks of Knight Island in the distance, and as the sun was setting we visualized silhouettes of faces along the top ridges. We could see indentations for eyes, large noses, and perfectly shaped lips. It was an incredibly beautiful view—we never got tired of it.

Unfortunately, we still had lots of mosquitoes in the cabin at night. We sprayed an insect repellent in the cabin and burned a powder called Buhach to try to keep them away. However, my face continued to have swollen and itchy welts every morning.

One morning when we went to start the boat, the battery was dead. Turk and Don poked around the control panel and the motor. Using the ammeter, they discovered that a diode malfunctioned. We would not be able to fix it until we got back to Cordova. However, we searched the shed and, fortunately, found a gas operated battery charger. From then on we would have to periodically charge the boat battery.

In contrast to the dreary, rainy stretch of weather that we had the whole time in Nelson Bay, our weather at Green Island was spectacularly sunny and dry. This put us all in a good mood. It almost seemed odd to not have to wear rain gear every day. The downside, however, was that we ran out of water in our rain-collection bucket. We hunted around and eventually found a small stream in a bay nearby. Ancel had named this little bay, "Log Cabin Bay" (fig. 2), because years ago he found remnants of a small building near this stream. The water was brown in color due to tannic acid from the roots of the trees. We had no choice but to collect the "tea water," bring it back to the cabin, and boil it before drinking it. We tried to go over to Knight Island (twelve miles away), which would certainly have fresh water streams coming off the glaciers, but the sea was too rough and we had to turn around.

On the evening of July 19, a floatplane arrived with our first drop-off of groceries and supplies. Also aboard were two Russian scientists, Lev and Popov. Don had met them at a conference and invited them to Green Island. One of the Russians did not speak English and the other one spoke only a little English. They gave us Olympic pins because the Olympics had just begun in Moscow. The United States and thirty-five other countries boycotted the Olympics due to the Soviet Union's invasion of Afghanistan. If we tried to discuss the political situation in the Soviet Union, one of the Russians flatly stated, "We left our camera in Moscow." It was obvious that politics was a taboo subject to discuss.

We did not catch any otters the next morning, and the water was like glass, so we took a boat ride to visit the Needle (fig. 1), a pinnacle of rock nine miles south of Green Island. Approximately three hundred Steller sea lions live on these rocks. We stopped the boat and as we drifted by the rocks, one sea lion after another jumped off the rocks, did belly flops into the ocean, and surrounded our boat. They made very loud growling sounds, like the noise one would make if imitating a monster. I realized that if any of us fell in the water we would be torn to shreds by their massive canines. We took several pictures.

Afterward, we went east to Montague Island (another five miles). On our way there, a black humpback whale surfaced just thirty feet from our boat! It spouted and a gush of water shot twenty feet into the air. Then it dove back down. Two other humpback whales did the same thing, although they were further away from us. We were happy to be in a boat that, although small, was very stable. We also saw fifteen minke whales, which are about half the size of humpbacks. They came close to our boat, surfaced, and took shallow dives over and over again. A short time later, a group of eight Dall's porpoises began bow-riding our wake. These six-foot long, black and white "mini-killer whales" sliced through the surface of the water with a ripping sound, as they caught a quick breath, and splashed up a spray of water in what seemed like an intentional show for us. Our final sightings of marine mammals of the afternoon were a group of harbor seals hauled out on rocks, which squirmed toward the water as we got close. Each appeared to be a slightly different shade of mottled gray, black, tan, and white, which varied individually and also by how dry they were. When a harbor seal was in the water we only saw its shiny head and big brown eyes. They seemed so mellow until they got caught in a net.

We stopped on Montague Island and saw four deer on the beach. We walked within fifty feet of them and they continued grazing on the beach grass. We spent some time walking the beach looking for "treasures" that may have washed ashore.

When we returned to Green Island there were no otters in the nets, only a small harbor seal. This one was smaller than the last one and we were able to get it out fairly easily with only minor cutting of the net and then some vigorous shaking.

When we finished checking nets we headed back to Camp Cove. Our boat mooring here was different from the one in Nelson Bay. The mooring was anchored near the center of the cove, one hundred yards from shore. We clipped the Boston Whaler to a floating buoy. To get to it, we would row out in a small rowboat that was kept on the beach, and then tie the rowboat to the buoy. Today, when we got to the mooring in the Whaler and went to untie the rowboat, the rope was tangled in kelp. I let go of the rope to get the kelp off of the buoy and the rowboat started drifting away. Before anyone could react, one of the Russians stripped down to his underpants and dove in the water to get it. We heard a shriek as he hit the fifty-five-degree water. However, he was able to swim to the rowboat, climb in, and row back to us. Turk and I looked at each other, both thinking the same thing—we could have just driven the Whaler to catch the rowboat! Oh well, it was a heroic effort. We then hooked the Whaler on the mooring and rowed to shore.

The next day we captured a thirty-eight-pound female in a net. We decided to name her "Olga" in honor of the Russians. At first we thought she was a very young otter, because she was so small, but we soon realized that she was an adult. Her teeth had a lot of wear and she had scars on her nose from previously breeding. After we drugged her, she had seizures and I had to give her Narcan to stop them. She woke up without any problems and swam off when we released her.

Later that day, we moved a net to Camp Cove to try to catch Crazy Otto. He appeared to be watching our every move when we walked along the beach, as well as when we took the boat out every day. Our mooring was right in the middle of his territory, which, he may have thought, was a rude intrusion on his future breeding opportunities.

The silver salmon were jumping everywhere in Camp Cove, so after supper the Russians decided they would try to catch some with their bare hands, apparently as a sort of challenge. I offered them some insect repellent, but Popov pinched his cheek and asserted confidently, "No problem—special Russian skin." A few minutes later we looked out the cabin window and saw the Russians wading in the water over the top of their hip boots, reaching out trying to catch salmon as they leaped out of the water. Later, the Russians came in the cabin with no fish, but their faces were full of welts that were bleeding from the bites of the white socks (small flies). We all laughed hard and joked back to them, "Special Russian skin!" They looked in the mirror and were shocked to see their faces. After a good laugh, they commented, "Your hip boots have holes in them! Our feet and pants are soaked!" Turk joked, "Yeah, there's the one big hole at the top that you put your foot in. The idea is not to wade out deeper than that."

Don, Nancy, and the Russians left Green Island the next morning. The floatplane from Chitina Air that came to get them brought us more groceries. When I unpacked them I found that we were given six pounds of cheese instead of the 0.6 pounds of cheese that I had ordered. Since we had no refrigeration we had to eat it fairly quickly—cheese for breakfast, cheese sandwiches for lunch, and cheese for snacks. We paid the price over the next few days when we each had constipation. Turk teased me for being too exact—"Instead of half a pound, you had to order 0.6 pounds!" I responded, "I thought you wanted your field assistant to be exact at all times."

The next day was our tenth day in a row of sunshine. It was great for working, but bad for our water supply. In the afternoon, we went to the stream in Log Cabin Bay, washed ourselves, and put some water in containers to bring back to the cabin. But even that was hard, as the stream was getting very shallow. We also spent a lot of time radiotracking. We saw three females with pups and four other individual otters.

That night we turned on the radio in the cabin because at 7:05 PM a radio station read messages, called "northwinds," to people in the bush. Anyone could call in a message to the radio station. We heard, "To Turk and Judy on Green Island, the Russians made it to Seattle and I left your warehouse key at the Reluctant Fisherman for you to pick up." It was from Don. We jumped up and down with excitement at receiving our first northwind.

The next day we caught a forty-pound female otter. She was clearly an adult, but she did not have a pup and was not lactating, indicating that she did not give birth this year. From this we learned that adult females do not necessarily give birth every year.

After supper, when we checked nets, we saw a male and female together in a very secluded cove that Ancel had named "Southeast Bay" (fig. 2). We put the boat on the beach and watched the otters through the binoculars. The male had a white head and he followed the female wherever she swam. He would dive every time she dove and swam right beside her. When she was on her stomach he grabbed her nose in his mouth and got on top of her back. She was only half his size. They copulated for fifteen seconds. Afterwards they groomed themselves and continued to swim side by side. The mosquitoes got so bad that we could not watch them any longer.

We had chosen Green Island as a study site because it was a female area for sea otters and we wanted to compare this to the male area (in northeast Prince William Sound). We planned to study the sea otter's social organization, feeding habits, and breeding behaviors. Although the peak-breeding season is in September and October, we wanted to learn what was happening prior to that time. We just learned that some mating occurs as early as mid-July.

Although Green Island is a female area, we were particularly interested in the small number of males that were here. All of them seemed to be large, mainly white-headed, and spread apart, each in a small bay or inlet. They appeared to be establishing territories, which would play a part in the upcoming breeding season. We used the Questar telescope to watch the otters from the beach. We could identify the male in Northeast Bay because he had a white tag in his right flipper and a yellow tag in his left. Ancel had captured him several years before. In Southeast Bay, there was a huge male with a hole in each flipper from previous tags that had come out. Ancel called him "Big Brute." Then there was Crazy Otto in Camp Cove. He had never been captured, but we could identify him by a distinct scar on his nose that we could only see looking through the telescope. In Log Cabin Bay there was a male whose head color was mixed brown and white, indicating that he was not as old as the others. There was also a male between Log Cabin Bay and Southeast Bay, and another smaller, dark-headed otter at the entrance to Log Cabin Bay. Every day we searched and recorded the location of each of these males, if we could find them. We hoped that we would be able to catch and put transmitters on several of them.

While the weather was so great we took time to enjoy the beautiful wildlife all around us. The birds were incredible. We regularly saw Steller's jays, Arctic loons, tufted puffins, marbled murrelets, harlequin ducks, and black oystercatchers. The oystercatchers are shorebirds that are sixteen inches tall, have a black body, thick pink legs, long orange bill, and yellow eyes with an orange ring around them. Often, while we were watching otters through the telescope, we would hear the oystercatchers' alarm call, an accelerating series of loud *wheep-wheeps*, as they strutted around the beach. We liked to zoom in on them with the Questar and watch them forage on the small animal life in the gravel and on the kelp.

Another interesting bird in this area was the dipper. They are small, drab, gray birds that have the capability of being able to walk, while fully submerged, on the bottom of a stream for thirty seconds at a time as they pluck away at aquatic larvae. After coming out of the water they like to stand on a rock and pump their body up and down, hence giving them the name "dipper."

My birthday came and Turk surprised me. He brought a cake mix to Green Island and made me a cake in the oven of the oil stove. It came out great, despite the fact that the temperature in the oil stove was hard to maintain and it frequently rose over four hundred degrees. He also gave me some beautiful walrus ivory earrings that he had purchased in Cordova. We felt like we were the only two people in the world living on this uninhabited island. Although Turk was very romantic, he did not express it in his field notes. He simply wrote, "Jude's birthday. No otters captured."

On July 25 we caught our first female and pup at the 10:00 PM net check. We drugged the mother, but handled the pup without drugs. The pup squalled the whole time that we were working on its mother. The pup kept nibbling at its mother and touching her with its forepaws, trying to wake her up. The mother weighed fifty-two pounds and had a white head. The male pup weighed eighteen pounds. We put a transmitter on both of them. When the mother began waking up from the drug she grabbed her pup and hugged him around the neck with her forepaws. She then groomed the pup's fur. When she was fully awake, she scampered over the side of the boat, followed by the pup, but when they hit the water they inadvertently headed in different directions. Despite being nearly pitch black, the mother sensed that the pup had gone the other way.

She quickly swam to her pup, grabbed him with her forepaws, and swam away on her back with him on her chest.

After working up the female and pup we had to check one more net. We could barely see our way. Suddenly, we heard a loud noise and felt the boat jerk. Our motor hit a rock. It kept running so we did not stop to look at it. We made it back to the cabin at 12:15 AM. We inspected the motor and there was a dent in the skeg below the prop, and the prop was ruined.

The next day Turk changed the prop. We were prepared and brought a spare one with us to Green Island. We radiotracked and checked the nets. We caught another harbor seal in the net in Northwest Bay. We figured we should take the net out of that bay because there were big rocks that we could hit on the way to check the net, and Turk and I continually disagreed on the safest route to approach this bay. Moreover, the water was quite a bit rougher here and we kept catching harbor seals.

We started seeing some different males in the anchorage and realized that the territories were still in a state of flux. We could easily identify males by their penile ridge when they rested on their backs. Conversely, for females we could see their two abdominal nipples, especially when their fur was wet.

That night it finally rained. It continued for several days so our water collection bucket was overflowing, and we filled other small buckets as a reserve supply. Silver salmon were still jumping frequently out of the water in Camp Cove. Red thimbleberries were ripening on the bushes around the cabin. They were twice the size of a raspberry and had much bigger seeds. Although they tasted good, the seeds got stuck in our teeth.

We had lots of dirty laundry so one afternoon when it wasn't raining we went to the stream in Log Cabin Bay. We washed our clothes and had to hang them all over the inside of the cabin to dry because it was threatening to rain again. We noticed that Crazy Otto was not in Camp Cove, but we saw a white-headed otter on the outside of the spit (fig. 2) and figured it must be him. We still had no luck catching him.

The rain returned along with a strong wind. The two of us had been alternating checking the nets at 4:00 AM, but this morning we decided to do it together because the water was so rough. The nets had twisted a lot and became severely tangled. We went back to the cabin to get some breakfast before facing the chore of untangling them. Later in the morning we had the patience to untangle the four nets, each taking over an hour.

We continued to radiotrack, check the tracking station, and do feeding observations. Crazy Otto came back into Camp Cove and we watched him feed for twenty minutes. He would consistently dive for about seventy seconds and come to the surface with more than one butter clam. While lying on his back he would use his forepaws to rub and twist a clamshell, thereby splitting it open. Then, grasping it in his teeth, he would pull his neck back, causing the clam to stretch and separate from the shell. After each bite he would roll to his left or right side, sometimes totally rolling over to wash the bits of clamshell off his chest. When he finished one clam he would reach under his armpit and pull out another. He remained on the surface for thirty-five to sixty seconds and would then periscope vertically up in the water, and dive down. The periscoping behavior fascinated us. We developed two theories to explain it. One was that it gave them more leverage to dive as their upper body was fully above the water. Alternately, they used it as a way to locate exactly where they were feeding using landmarks on shore. This way they could assess whether to come back to this spot again. We noticed that each time they periscoped, they looked around in several directions before they dove.

A highlight of the day occurred when we heard a floatplane approaching. We were off radiotracking and raced back to Camp Cove as the plane was landing. The pilot gave us our groceries and mail. We received letters from family and it was great to read the news.

When we were radiotracking at 8:00 PM, we noticed that there was a female and pup caught in the net in Southeast Bay. When we got closer to the net we saw that the pup was very small and had not actually been caught. It was floating approximately ten feet from its mother and was crying out very loudly. Apparently, the mother had just been caught. If we did not arrive there at that time, the young pup might have floated away. The female was splashing and thrashing trying to get out of the net. She did not pay any attention to her pup until we pulled the net closer to the pup. Then she nibbled at her pup and continued to thrash in the net. We drugged the female and brought both otters on board the boat after she went to sleep. The pup kept squalling loudly. We tried to calm it down by rubbing and blowing air into its fur to try to keep it warm. We eventually covered the pup in one of our heavy floatation coats, put it beside its mother, and it finally settled down.

The female weighed fifty-five pounds and the pup only weighed seven and one-half pounds and was twenty-four inches long. The pup was probably only two-weeks-old. It had yellow-brown fur, very small forepaws, and a bushy tail. We did not put any tags or transmitter on the pup due to its small size. When the female was still drugged she reached for her pup with her forepaws whenever the pup yelled out, but then she fell back to sleep. When the female woke up after we gave her the Narcan, we placed the pup in the water. The pup floated in the water and the female jumped in, grabbed the pup with her forepaws, and swam away on her back. We watched them for fifteen minutes. When the female let go of the pup it was unable to swim and wiggled its hind flippers and body in the water. It looked very uncoordinated.

The next day was sunny and warm. At the first morning net check we found that one of the nets was snagged on some submerged rocks. We could not free it until five hours later when it was low tide. If any otters had been caught they would have drowned because the lead line was stuck and they would not have been able to float to the surface. Subsequently, we moved the net.

In the afternoon, we observed otters for three hours through the Questar telescope. We saw three different females with pups and the pups were all at different developmental stages. The first pup was unable to dive but was able to swim. When its mother dove for food, the pup floated on its back, put its chin in the air, arched its back, and put the top of its head underwater so it could try to see its mother. Then it rolled onto its stomach and put its head underwater to watch its mother get food.

The second pup could only dive about one-foot deep. It would lie on its stomach and try to dive over and over again, but it kept bobbing to the surface. When its mother came up, the pup would nurse while she was eating. It was too big to lie on its mother's chest so it floated perpendicular to her body in the water and sucked on her nipple.

The third pup could dive for eight to thirteen seconds and sometimes it actually came to the surface with food. All three pups tried to grab food from their mothers or tried to solicit food by putting their heads right next to their mothers' mouths. This prompted the mothers to give up some food. Often, a mother would purposely surface a short distance from her pup so she could eat some food herself before the pup could swim to her. We recognized that it was certainly labor-intensive for females to raise their pups.

The next day we observed a different female and pup feeding. This pup could swim on its stomach, but when it tried to dive, its buttocks would stay floating on top of the water while its head was underwater—like a person trying to dive with a tube around their waist.

We caught another harbor seal in a net the next morning. It had twisted so many times that the corks were all above its head and it could not come up to the surface to breathe, so it had drowned. We felt really bad.

Later that day, we spent hours observing otters through the telescope and spotting scope. We saw some otters feed on Helmet (*Telmessus*) crabs and clams. Unlike the large Dungeness crabs that we had seen in Nelson Bay, Helmet crabs were small (two-to three-inch shell), soft, and easy for the otters to handle. They ate everything but the shell.

We also recorded the location of all territorial males. They did not remain in their small territories, but rather swam throughout the anchorage during the day. One male otter was resting in a bay as another otter entered. The resting male swam away from the approaching otter, so he must have known the other otter was a more dominant male. If it had been a female, he would have tried to entice her to stay with him. At night the males stayed in their territories. Each evening they would swim on their backs around the perimeter of their territory while grooming their chests with their forepaws. We called this the "territorial patrol."

The following day we were walking up to the tracking station and noticed that the small bushes along the trail were covered with large, plump, blueberries. We decided to pick them. We could not resist eating handfuls as we collected them. When we got back to the cabin, I placed them in a bowl and planned to make a pie after supper. When I went to wash them off after dinner, however, there was a scum of one-quarter-inch white and brown worms crawling all over the side of the bowl, and many still emerging from the blueberries. All we could picture in our minds were the worms crawling around in our stomachs. I looked around the cabin and found some Canadian Mist whiskey. We chugged it straight, hoping to kill the worms in our stomachs! Of course, Turk makes no mention of this in his field notes. I could not cook with the berries after that and ended up throwing them out. We later learned that Alaskans soak the berries in salt water to get the worms to crawl out before eating them.

Every day our observations taught us more about the otters and also raised more questions. At low tide we found numerous shells of butter clams. In virtually every pair, one of the shells and hinge were intact, but a small piece was missing from the second shell. We originally thought the shells had broken from being thrashed by wave action on the rocky beach. However, as we made more observations of foraging otters, we came to realize that all these shells were the result of otters biting into them when they were feeding. We made a collection of these otter-cracked shells so we could determine the size distribution of the clams that the otters were selecting. We then collected live clams within this same size distribution in order to measure the amount of meat that otters were consuming. We also preserved some of these clams so that Turk could later determine their caloric value.

The wildlife continued to amaze us. When I was radiotracking, I frequently saw minke whales and porpoises in the water, and many harbor seals hauled out on the rocks by Northwest Bay. There was a family of Steller's jays that consisted of two adults and two young birds living by the cabin. I fed them bread every day hoping

I could get them to eat out of my hand like those in Olsen Bay, but they never did. When we did observations from one small island in Gibbon Anchorage we saw sea urchins, hermit crabs, limpets, and mussels in the intertidal pools. We flipped over a sea urchin and watched it easily turn itself back over.

According to Ancel, the breeding season does not peak until September, but we saw several matings in August. Unexpectedly, females bred even while with their pup. I saw the male in Log Cabin Bay swim up to a female and tumble with her. They both swam to the back of the bay while a smaller otter followed them porpoising the whole way. The smaller otter was approximately twenty-five pounds and appeared to be the female's pup. The male grabbed the female's nose and got on her back and they copulated. Afterwards, they groomed themselves and then all three otters rested together.

By August 7 it was dark from 11:00 PM to 3:30 AM. Turk liked to track all night and did this on several occasions. He was able to collect data on dive times and surface times by listening to radio-signals when the otters were feeding. We compared his data to the data on the automatic tracking station and it correlated perfectly for those otters that were eating close to the station. Turk tracked one female otter that fed in one place and then moved to another. He measured the depth and discovered that dive times were longer when she fed in deeper water, but were remarkably consistent at a given depth. Surface times remained the same, irrespective of depth, for each type of food.

Many times when Turk tracked all night, I read in the cabin. I learned that harbor seals are born from June to mid-July and weigh twenty-eight pounds at birth. They can swim immediately and double their birth weight in one month. That meant that the harbor seal that died in the net was probably only one-week-old because it weighed thirty-five pounds.

The narrow finger, or spit, of land jutting out from across the cabin was a prime spot for us to do observations. Ancel had built a small, wooden blind near the tip of the spit for just this purpose. The blind was a four-by-four-by-five-foot high plywood box that stood on five-foot stilts. A section of the front and sides could be opened to observe the otters. The main benefit of the blind was that we could get out of the wind and rain while doing observations through the telescope.

One sunny afternoon we were doing observations from near the tip of the spit. We did not use the blind because the weather was so nice. As I was watching an otter foraging through the telescope, I saw a boat go floating by. I noticed that it was a Boston Whaler with no people in it. "Boy, that's odd," I thought to myself. "Whose boat is that, and where are the people?" It took me a moment to realize that it was our boat! Suddenly the cold chill of panic set in. "Turk, oh no! Our boat!" Turk looked up from the clipboard and said, "What now?"

Anchoring the boat while we did observations from shore was always a tricky proposition. If the tide was coming in, we buried the anchor above the high tide mark. If the tide was going out, we had to make sure that the boat would not get beached by anchoring it slightly off shore. The difficult part was to have the anchor far enough from shore to keep the boat from getting beached, but close enough that we could paddle the back end of the boat closer to shore and get out. On this day, the tide was going out and the wind was blowing strongly off shore. That made it nice because it kept the boat from washing up on the beach.

We hadn't realized, however, that the wind had substantially picked up because we were doing observations from a sheltered area on the other side of the spit, out of sight of the boat. The anchor dragged loose and the boat drifted away. It was too far away for us to swim to, but even if it was closer, the water was only fifty degrees. We would have become hypothermic. We ran back to the cabin trying to think of a way to get to the rowboat that was moored in the middle of Camp Cove. We had the idea of building a raft using some empty fifty-five-gallon gas drums. We grabbed two empty drums from the shed, tied them together with rope, and then set a piece of plywood on top. Fortunately, there was also an old paddle in the shed. Initially, Turk thought he would kneel on the plywood and paddle out to the rowboat. However, he immediately realized that it was much too tippy. Instead, he lay on his stomach on top of the plywood, and paddled in front of him.

He found that he had to use short, choppy, strokes pulling toward him. If he pulled too hard, the makeshift raft tilted and he started to slide off the front.

Since the wind was blowing hard from right to left, we had launched the raft well down the beach to assure that Turk could make it to the mooring without getting blown out of Camp Cove. However, his forward progress was much slower than expected and the raft was not heading at the anticipated angle. It became clear to me that he wasn't going to make it. In fact, I kept yelling: "You're going to miss it!" Turk later said to me that my "coaching" was not helpful. He was already in a panic about not being able to reach the mooring and floating out to sea on a couple of gas drums. He did, however, with some furious stroking, just make it to the rowboat, and came to pick me up on shore. We rowed as fast as we could, but when we got to the end of the spit we saw no sign of the Whaler. We knew that if we had to paddle the rowboat outside of the anchorage we would be in trouble because we could see large whitecaps in the distance. As we headed that way, with a very sick feeling in our stomachs, we came around the backside of Island Two and saw the boat sitting in the lee of the wind. The anchor had, fortunately, snagged on some eelgrass. We climbed into the Whaler, towed the rowboat back to the mooring, and then towed the gas-can raft to shore. Once we were safely back at the cabin we realized how dire this situation could have been. If the boat had gone out to sea we would have been stranded.

The next day we went out to the tip of the spit again, but this time after we set the anchor, we ran another safety rope from the boat to a tree on shore. We saw Big Brute and Crazy Otto within fifty yards of each other. They were not aggressive and totally ignored one another. They did not act protective of any certain area of the anchorage. We thought this might change in September when the breeding season would be at its peak.

Otto began feeding and came up with two Helmet crabs. He put one crab upside down on his chest so it wouldn't run off while he leisurely ate the other one. Then he ate the second crab.

We noticed that the otters seemed to be able to smell our presence. If we were downwind from them they did not notice us, but if we were upwind they quickly detected us and swam further away. I wonder if it had anything to do with our infrequent showers.

When we radiotracked later in the day we saw a female and pup near one of the nets. We tried to chase them into the net with the boat. When they were five feet from the net the female dove down and the pup tried to follow her. After taking two small dives, the pup got caught in the net. Suddenly, the female grabbed the pup from underwater, pulled it out of the net, and came to the surface thirty yards away.

We got into a dry stretch in terms of catching otters, but a wet stretch in terms of the weather. We went nine days without catching any otters and without seeing the sun. We took turns getting up for the first morning net check, but our alarm clock broke. When it was my turn to get up first, I did not sleep well knowing I had to wake up without the alarm. It was so hard to force myself to get out of the warm sleeping bag at 5:00 AM when I heard rain pounding on the corrugated tin roof of the cabin. However, I gloated when it was Turk's turn. On one of those days, Turk was gone for an unusually long time, which meant something was up. I could hear the drone of the motor coming down Camp Cove. If it came up to the beach in front of the cabin it would mean he needed help with something, such as an otter, large harbor seal, or some issue with the net. Today, though, the sound of the motor stayed off shore. In a few minutes I could hear him rowing to shore and dragging the rowboat up the beach. It meant I could stay in my sleeping bag—I felt a little guilty because I was happy about that, and wondered if Turk felt the same when I was out checking nets. When he came in the cabin he told me he released two baby harbor seals from a net. Later that day we caught another one.

Our days consisted of checking nets four times, starting at 5:00 AM, checking the automatic tracking station, radiotracking in and around the anchorage, and doing observations from either the spit, Island Three, or Island Four. We would eat lunch and supper in the cabin and took turns cooking supper. We spent a lot of time discussing everything that we saw and we each made sure we identified individual otters when we saw them, and corroborated our identifications with each other afterward.

On August 10 we did observations from Island Four and saw Otto, who we identified by his nose scar, swim on his stomach over to a female in Log Cabin Bay. They rolled together a couple of times and it was apparent that the female was unreceptive to him so they split apart and swam off in different directions and groomed. Ten minutes later, Otto started swimming fast on his stomach as if he were approaching another female. An otter suddenly surfaced from underwater in front of Otto. They rolled together, grabbed each other with their forepaws, and splashed. This was not a courtship, but an act of aggression. Otto then chased the other otter, a male, to the back of Log Cabin Bay, as they were both porpoising. This was the first time that we had seen otters really fight (when they were not caught in a net).

Later that same day we did observations in Northwest Bay. We saw a female resting with a male, plus four other otters, feeding. One of the otters came to the surface with a three-inch butter clam and a flat rock that was five inches wide. It placed the rock on its chest and pounded the butter clam on it to open the shells. Then the otter dropped the rock back into the water when it dove. Whenever this otter surfaced with a butter clam, it also surfaced with a rock, but when it came up with a crab, it didn't. We found it interesting that tools would only be used with certain clams.

On August 11 we radiotracked and saw a female and pup near a net but they were not caught. Desperate at not having caught any otters in many days, we decided to make an attempt to chase them into the net. The female kept diving, and would sometimes grab her pup and other times leave the pup on the surface of the water. Once when she left her pup on the surface we zipped the boat over to it and Turk grabbed it by the tail. At the same time, the pup dove and, unfortunately, the tail slipped out of Turk's hands. Unable to slow the boat down quickly enough, we went right over the pup. Luckily, the prop did not hit the pup, and it was not harmed. We stopped the chase after this because we were afraid that the female would abandon her pup or we might harm it—back to the drawing board on that technique.

We pulled the nets out of the water after that because we were going to go to Cordova the next day. We wore rubber gloves because the nets were full of jellyfish. Neither of us got stung. In order to take the net out of the water, one of us grabbed the line with corks while the other grabbed the lead line and we slowly pulled it into the bow of the boat onto a tarp, trying to keep it from getting tangled. After getting a net in the boat, we drove to shore near the cabin and schlepped it into the shed.

After supper we filled some six-gallon cans with gas, took down the tracking station (not the antennas), and charged the boat battery. It took us all evening to pack and prepare for our long boat ride to Cordova. We planned to return to Green Island for the September breeding season, but first we wanted to check on our otters in Nelson Bay. We were nervous about the ride knowing we had to cross the ocean entrance and that the battery was draining and not recharging. This turned out to be only a minor issue compared to the problem that we would soon encounter.

Cabin on Green Island

Floatplane delivering groceries

Harbor seals hauled out on rocks

The Blind

# Hello Coast Guard—It's Us Again

We woke up the next morning at 4:30 AM. It was cloudy with poor visibility so we took our time finishing packing and cleaning up the cabin. We left Green Island at 7:30 AM. The sea was surprisingly calm, even as we crossed the Hinchinbrook Entrance. However, we cut the corner around Hinchinbrook Island too close and hit a shallow mud bar. Fortunately, the motor kept running. We arrived in Cordova at 10:00 AM. We inspected the motor at the dock and found that only a little paint had been rubbed off the prop.

In Cordova we did a lot of errands, shopped for groceries, stopped at the post office, and received lots of great mail from our families. Every place we went in town we were stopped by local people who asked how the otters were doing!

Since we had only three weeks before we would return to Green Island, we decided not to go through the hassle of setting up the Nelson Bay tent camp. Instead, we stayed at our trailer. This decision satisfied me, as I was not looking forward to dealing with the bears again.

The next day we did laundry and ran into a crewmember from the *Enforcer*, the boat that had brought us gas on Green Island. He asked us about our study. The pay showers at the laundromat were closed so we went back to the Forest Service bunkhouse to use the shower. At the bunkhouse there were three women, whom we had never met, who knew about our study.

Later that day, we radiotracked in Nelson Bay and could not find many of our transmittered otters. We set up the automatic tracking station in the same spot as before. The mosquitoes and "no see-ums" were awful, and despite wearing hats with nets to keep away the bugs, they still bit our necks.

When we radiotracked the next day, we only saw a raft of sixty-five otters in Nelson Bay. We tried to drift up to them in the boat, but they swam away quickly, before we could get close to them. We wondered if there had been fishing boats in the bay that disturbed the otters when we were at Green Island.

We drove to Simpson Bay and found a raft of ninety otters in a protected cove in the back of the bay. There were no otters here before we went to Green Island. We observed the otters through the telescope and identified several tagged individuals. The raft of otters was very active and, although we presumed that most or all of them were males, they were doing the mating behavior with each other! Several otters were biting each other's noses, they nibbled at one another's groins, they vocalized loudly, and we saw erect penises. Since we had not seen this behavior in June or July, we surmised that the male otters' testosterone levels were increased in preparation for the breeding season. However, these males were too young to breed.

We took the boat to Sheep Bay and found fifty-five otters. In May we only counted thirty otters here. We guessed that several otters left Port Gravina and went to Sheep Bay, and some of them continued east to Simpson Bay. Now that the breeding season was close, young male otters may have been forced to leave Port Gravina because the territorial males kicked them out.

When we got back to our trailer that night we decided to visit the new Forest Service district ranger, Fred. Fred asked us what we planned to do with the trailer, and in the next breath made it clear that he wanted us to move it to another place outside the Forest Service compound. He had only been in Alaska for six weeks and already wanted us out! He said our trailer was blocking his loading zone. We told him about our deal with Dick Groff, but he brushed it off. We panicked and figured we'd better ask Dick for advice.

We went to the Cordova Outboard motor shop the next day

and bought a diode for the motor. We had received a check in the mail from the University of Minnesota so we had the funds to pay for it. We still had to be very frugal when spending money so our funding would last until the end of October. We did not buy any personal gear with project funds because we would have run out of money. We even tried to eat cheaper food to spare the budget. In fact, we limited ourselves to a dessert of only two cookies a day. We replaced the diode, lubricated the motor, and hoped that our boat would now charge the battery and run smoothly. Maybe our boat problems were now behind us.

We spent the rest of the day radiotracking in Nelson Bay. When we returned to our trailer that night we had no water. A water pipe in the warehouse that was connected to our trailer had frozen the night before. This was amazing—it was August! We had to haul water from the warehouse in order to cook, and we had to do dishes and wash up in the warehouse.

We continued to radiotrack daily in Simpson Bay, Nelson Bay, and Orca Inlet. We counted and mapped the locations of all rafts. We checked the automatic tracking station regularly and often found that it had stopped working. It seemed like each time it quit, it was due to a problem that we had never encountered before. We were constantly cleaning the pens, tweaking the wind-up clock, lubricating the gears, fixing a paper jam, or tuning the receiver, all while fighting the voracious bugs. We often found bear scats on the steps that we had carved in the hill up to the tracking station. It seemed like we set up our station on a walkway for bears!

We continued to do observations of otters and identified individuals on a regular basis. We often saw sea otters biting at their transmitters and also saw some otters with their transmitters missing. They had slits in the webbing of their flippers where the transmitters had come off. This was quite a disappointment.

One day when we were in Cordova we saw Craig (the fisherman/biologist) and decided to go out with him and his wife at night. We went to the Black Sheep again and had a nice time. They introduced us to a professor from the University of Alaska and then we were all invited to the professor's house one evening to discuss sea otters and show slides.

The next time we saw Fred at the Forest Service we explained our situation with the trailer and contract with Dick. We told him the contract should be in his files. He was much more understanding this time and just asked us to move the trailer away from the loading dock. We were quite relieved.

On August 18, Turk's uncle, Louis, came to visit us. He was taking a tour of Alaska with a group and broke away for twenty-four hours to see us. After spending the night in our trailer we took Louis radiotracking in Nelson Bay. We had a beautiful sunny day. We saw lots of rafting otters, harbor seals hauled out on rocks, salmon swimming up a stream, and bald eagles. It was fun to share this experience with a family member.

The next day we decided to take the boat to Hinchinbrook Island to observe sea otters where we had seen them hauled out on a mud bar from the airplane. We radiotracked on the way there and found three otters that we had caught in Nelson Bay, which further supported our theory about the otters knowing their way around northeast Prince William Sound. As we were driving in Orca Inlet toward Hinchinbrook Island, we were worried about getting stuck in the mud again, because it was unclear where the deep channel was. Then we saw a big boat ahead and decided to go toward it, thinking that it must have been traveling in the channel. We suddenly ground to a halt as the motor hit the mud bar. Fortunately, we were traveling slowly enough that we did not get stuck. We used paddles to push ourselves off and return to deeper water. As we looked ahead at the big boat we realized that it was stuck in the mud and the channel was two hundred feet away from us!

Once we arrived at Hinchinbrook Island we climbed up a steep rocky bank and found a flattened grassy area to observe otters through the telescope and spotting scope. There were ninety otters hauled out on the mud and thirty-six otters in the water in a raft nearby. When an otter hauled out of the water it swam up to the edge of the mud, reached up with its forepaws and then hopped up on the mud. On land, the otters were very awkward. Their flippers, while adapted well for swimming in the water, were very clumsy for walking. Moreover, their hind legs were so much longer than their forelegs that they hobbled in a hunched position. It seemed like a great struggle.

Some otters on the mud were resting, yet most of them were interacting with each other. One otter would hop over to another one and bite its nose or grab it with forepaws. We saw three different interactions where two otters fought with each other for approximately ten seconds. We saw two of the otters that we had caught in Nelson Bay with tags, but no transmitters on their flippers. We realized that we had to design a better way to attach the radio-transmitter in the future.

The sea otters were particularly skittish on land. When a fishing boat drove near the mudflat they all hopped back in the water and formed a raft.

By 4:00 PM all the otters were off the mud bar and were feeding. We saw a male and female with an older pup (approximately twenty-five pounds) feeding close to each other. The male even gave some food to the pup when the pup swam over to it—however, we also saw the male steal food from the pup. After that happened, the female quickly grabbed her pup and swam away from the male. The male followed the female very closely, the same behavior we saw at Green Island prior to copulation. The male dove under the water every time the female dove. Once, when the female came up to the surface with food and the male did not have any, he just groomed himself while she ate and then dove down again when she dove. The pup often stayed on the surface when its mother dove. Both the female and pup pounded clams on their chests to open them, and one time the female surfaced with a rock to pound the clam on.

We were surprised to find these few maverick females in a male area, and even more surprised that a single male could court this female without being bothered by the many other testosterone-charged males nearby. It seemed apparent that this white-headed male, who was larger than most of the other males in this area, did not have a distinct territory but "owned" the moving area around the female.

We wanted to observe the otters in this area again the next day but it poured, and the fog was, as the fishermen liked to say, "pea soup." We knew we would not be able to find our way across the mud bar. We couldn't even radiotrack because the receiver got too wet and would not work, despite the fact that we always kept it in a plastic bag. We took it apart in the trailer hoping that if it dried out it would start to work again.

The following day, we decided to count otters in the different bays within Port Gravina. On the way there we noticed that the boat's steering seemed a bit weird—it would not respond at all to very small turns of the steering wheel, but then would respond all of a sudden when the steering wheel was cranked very far in one direction. Determined to "get the data," we forged on, thinking it was a minor glitch that we could fix later. When we got to our favorite place in Port Gravina, Hell's Hole, where we previously had narrowly escaped disaster, we lost all steering to the left. We had to negotiate our way out of the bay using a series of right turns. Shortly after getting out of Hell's Hole we lost all steering. Of course, by this time the wind had picked up and the waves were three feet high. We scrambled around the boat to find something that we could attach to the motor and steer from the stern. Initially, we tied a broken paddle to the motor, but it kept slipping off. Bobbing around among the whitecaps, being pushed toward the boulder beach, panic started to set in. It started to feel like we were on a raft made of two gas drums, once again, but this time without a paddle! We called the Coast Guard on the walkie-talkie and explained our situation. We half expected them to respond, "You guys again? Can't you stay out of trouble?" But, they were polite and helpful.

As I was talking to the Coast Guard, Turk took down our radiotracking antenna and used the U-bolt to fasten a steel rod that was lying in the boat to the base of the motor. This was secure enough for him to steer the boat as I controlled the throttle. However, the 85-hp motor had so much torque that we had to drive much slower than usual. It took us two and one-half hours to get back to Cordova while the Coast Guard periodically checked in with us. When we got to Cordova we took apart the steering mechanism and found a broken steering cable. Turk's field notes recounted the day this way, "Counts of otters not very good due to choppy water and broken steering."

Despite the broken cable, we did a lot of radiotracking the next day in Nelson Bay using the juried stern steering. It was a Sunday so the outboard shop was closed. We'd have to wait to buy a new steering cable, but meanwhile we wanted to be productive. The following day we found out that the outboard shop did not have the part and would have to order it from Anchorage. They said it would arrive the next day.

In the meantime, we needed to arrange some logistics to be able to work on Green Island again. We talked to the captain of the *Enforcer* to see if he would bring us more gas. However, he wasn't going to be in the area of Green Island until November. He told us to talk to the captain of the Alaska Department of Fish and Game boat, the *Montague*. The *Montague* was out, but would be back in Cordova in a few days. We also had to discuss our study with the Eyak Native Corporation because the director sent us a letter requesting a verbal report.

Many people in Cordova told us that the Dungeness crab season was closed due to a crash in the number of crabs. We went to the Alaska Department of Fish and Game and spoke to Al, the shellfish biologist in charge of setting the crab season. He told us that the population had taken a drastic decline this year in Nelson Bay. We told him we had seen 150 sea otters in Nelson Bay earlier this summer, that the otters ate an average of two crabs per hour, and they fed for ten hours a day. He was not aware that sea otters could affect the population of crabs. But it certainly seemed more than coincidental that as the otters moved into Nelson Bay the crab population plummeted. The crab numbers were still high in Orca Inlet, and the otters had just arrived there. Given the high number of otters we had seen on the mud bar, we predicted the crabs wouldn't last long. This was the first time the Dungeness crab season had been closed since 1960. Al was not ready to blame the low number of crabs this year entirely on sea otter predation. He explained to us that Dungeness crab populations are cyclical and he expected that they might rise again in a few years. However, this never happened. Nearly three decades later, otters have remained in this area, crab numbers have not rebounded, and the fishery has remained closed.

The Cordova outboard motor shop received our steering linkage so we fixed the boat. Afterwards, feeling good about having a working boat again, Turk decided to radiotrack all night. I went back to the trailer and planned to take over radiotracking early the next morning.

At 8:00 AM I took over radiotracking and also did observations through the telescope. The otters in rafts were very active—they bit each other's groins, bit noses, rolled together, and many of them had erect penises. They were clearly much more rambunctious than they were in June.

As I watched and collected feeding data, I found that I could determine if an otter was eating clams or crabs by its actions, even if I couldn't actually see the food item. With clams, they pounded them with their forepaws and then twisted their bodies in the water after they ate them. With crabs, they nibbled the legs and then ate the body. Also, the times on the surface of the water eating food items remained very consistent for a given type of food. If an otter came up from a dive with no food, it would spend time on the surface grooming before diving down again. I wondered if it needed this time to recover from the deep dives.

After watching foraging dives from shore, we would go out in the boat and measure the depth of the water where the otter was feeding. We marked a rope in increments of fifteen feet (actually, five meters), tied a rusty hammer on one end, and used it to sound the depth. The average depth of foraging dives in Nelson Bay was over ninety feet. The deepest successful foraging dive that we observed was 230 feet. We found a close correlation between the depth of the dive and the amount of time that the otter was submerged. One-third of the dives in Nelson Bay were more than two minutes long, and three dives exceeded three minutes. The physiological adaptations that enable otters to dive to these depths are quite remarkable. But even more astonishing is their ability to locate buried clams on the bottom of the ocean in the pitch dark. No one has yet figured out how they do this.

We continued radiotracking and observing otters every day. We checked the automatic tracking station daily because it continued to malfunction and required constant tweaking.

One evening, Dick Groff invited us over for dinner with his

wife, Kay, and daughter. After dinner Dick gave us some frozen Dungeness crabs that he had caught, to take back to our trailer. Although the commercial crab fishery was closed, subsistence fishing was still allowed.

The next day we had to finalize the arrangements for getting gas delivered to Green Island. The captain of the *Enforcer* told us his plans had changed and he could deliver five drums of gas to us. The captain of the *Montague* said he could transport ten drums. We were relieved to get these crucial arrangements finalized—it was now September 2 and we wanted to get to Green Island as soon as possible.

We were told by the captain of the *Montague* that the fish biologist at the Department of Fish and Game wanted to see us. We met with him and he asked us to count salmon in a stream on Green Island. We were amazed at how many people knew about us. We could not walk anywhere in town without someone asking us about the sea otters. We heard everyone's opinion of them. Some people thought they were cute, loving, animals. Fishermen hated them because they got caught in their nets. Crab fishermen also hated them because they "ate all the crabs." We were frequently asked if we would recommend a hunting season for otters!

After arranging all the logistics we were ready to head back to Green Island. We looked forward to the solitude of being there, and the excitement of gathering new biological information during the breeding season, but wondered what sort of adventures would lie ahead.

# Breeding Season on Green Island

On September 4 we packed up the boat and headed to Green Island. The water started out flat and we thought we were going to have an easy trip, but by the time we got to the Hinchinbrook Entrance the swells were six feet high! It took us almost four hours to get to Green Island and we used four and one-half cans of gas, one more full can than our previous trip. We always carried more gas than we thought we would need, and fortunately we never ran out.

When we walked up to the cabin, the padlock was cut off the door and lying on the ground. Someone had broken into the cabin but nothing was missing. Maybe they just needed a place to sleep.

After we unpacked the boat and got settled in the cabin, we decided to put one net in the water that evening, and put out three more the next day. That evening, standing on the beach in front of the cabin, we saw a single white-headed otter in Camp Cove. We set up the telescope to look for the nose scar, thinking it must be Crazy Otto, but it wasn't any otter that we recognized from the previous month. That really surprised us because Otto appeared to be king of Camp Cove when we were here in July and August.

At the 5:00 AM net check we were excited to see three otters in the net. That initial thrill was quickly quelled when we got closer to the net and noticed that two of the otters had been fighting.

We drugged those two and brought them on board. One was a fifty-eight-pound male and the other was a thirty-eight-pound female. They both had injuries from fighting. The male's nose was bleeding and his outside digit on his right flipper was bitten. The female had a bleeding nose and her right eye was swollen. We worked on the male first. We were concerned because his body temperature registered less than ninety degrees. His hair was saturated and matted down, and the cold water had penetrated to his skin. Normally, when an otter can groom its fur it will retain a layer of air that insulates the skin from the water. However, otters are unable to groom in the net, which is why it was important to check nets frequently. After we gave him the Narcan, he raised his head for one second and then went back to sleep on the bow of the boat. We wrapped him in a floatation coat and let him sleep while we worked up the other two otters.

The third otter had been caught one hundred feet from the other two otters so he was not involved in the fight. He weighed eighty-two pounds.

After releasing the female and the large male, we turned our attention to the smaller male who was still sleeping on the bow of the boat. Concerned about his hypothermia, we decided to try to warm him up back at the cabin. We carried him inside, placed him by the oil stove, and put a kerosene heater near him. We rubbed his fur with towels. His body temperature was still less than ninety degrees, pulse was eighty, and his respirations were twenty. A little over an hour later he died from hypothermia. We both felt sickened by this setback. A day that started on what seemed like a tremendous high had quickly turned to the lowest low. Sadly, we did a necropsy on him and did not find any other ailments that could have contributed to his death.

In the afternoon, we radiotracked the female that had been in the fight in the net. We found her hauled out on a beach. She was resting and occasionally grooming. She appeared weak. We walked up to her and took off her radio-transmitter because we did not want her to have the added stress of swimming with it on her flipper. She did not try to fight as we worked on her without drugs.

We watched her from a distance until 5:30 PM and she stayed on the beach the whole time.

The following day we went to the beach where she had been hauled out and she was gone. We figured that she swam away because her body would have washed up on the beach with the tide if she had died.

We radiotracked and found the big male that we caught yesterday in Southeast Bay. We named him "Duke." He turned out to be a key breeding male in the anchorage.

We set up the automatic tracking station and discovered that we had left some of the ink pens and the ink tray for the recorder in Cordova. We used the VHF radio in the cabin to call the U.S. Forest Service in Anchorage. We wanted to ask Ancel to contact a person at the Forest Service in Cordova to get the parts to the tracking station and bring them to Chitina Air so they could be flown to us with groceries and mail. We also had to report the dead otter. It took several tries to get through on the radio, but we eventually reached the secretary in Ancel's office.

The amount of daylight lessened dramatically each day. It was now dark from 8:00 PM to 5:00 AM. The weather also took a turn for the worse, as each day it rained hard and was incredibly windy. We dubbed it "pouring ass rain" or "PAR." We had five days in a row where we heard on the radio that there were small craft warnings in Prince William Sound, and even the water in Gibbon Anchorage was very rough.

Duke stayed in Southeast Bay and another big male came in to Camp Cove. A third male was in Northeast Bay. It appeared like the territories were becoming more fixed.

On September 10 at the 5:00 AM net check, we caught a sixty-nine-pound male and a thirty-seven-pound female in the same net. They were ten feet apart, were unable to fight, and were in great condition. We noticed that the *Enforcer* was anchored nearby so we drove over to them at 7:00 AM after working up the otters. The captain, Tom, was a wonderful man. We went aboard the boat, had coffee and Danish with him, and he gave us another goodie bag as we were leaving that contained milk, oranges, Danish, and turnovers. He told us he would bring us any supplies that we needed whenever he came by Green Island.

After breakfast the work began. The *Enforcer* had brought five fifty-five-gallon drums of gas for us. Each drum was loaded into our boat, one at a time via a winch, and five times we drove the boat to the beach in front of the cabin, pushed the drum out of the bow of the boat and into the water, and rolled it up the beach above the high tide mark. The whole time the weather was PAR.

Two hours later we heard a plane in the distance and it landed on floats in front of the cabin. It was Chitina Air with our groceries, mail, and parts for the automatic tracking station. I gave the pilot a letter to mail to the grocery store with our shopping list when he got back to Cordova. This time I ordered "½-pound" of cheese so we would avoid the constipation problem (although I never told Turk that I caved in to his idea).

That afternoon we did some laundry. We filled a large metal basin with water and heated it up on the oil stove. We added laundry detergent and then our clothes. After some soaking and scrubbing we rinsed the clothes in cold water and hung them all over the cabin to dry. The one good thing about the rain was that we had an unlimited water supply.

During the late afternoon, after radiotracking and untangling net, we observed otters again. It was always fun watching females and pups feeding. One female gave her pup food from every dive until the pup was full, then the pup rested on the surface while the female continued to feed herself. As we watched these otters, we saw a river otter with four babies swim by. The river otters mainly used the freshwater ponds and streams on the island, but we occasionally saw them catching fish or eating small shellfish in the anchorage.

The next morning we caught a forty-eight-pound female. We noticed that the vaginas of the females were now pink compared to the gray color in the previous months. This was due to the hormonal changes associated with estrus.

We saw Duke try to interact with a feeding female but she paid no attention to him and kept eating. After fifteen minutes they swam away from each other. Apparently, she was not yet in estrus.

We watched another female and pup feeding for over half an hour. This pup would leap in the air and dive when its mother dove, but it rarely came to the surface with any food. Twice it surfaced with a large clam and it appeared proud to have found a clam bigger than its mother's. However, when it opened it up it was full of mud. The female frequently gave food to the pup, but sometimes she would surface far enough away from the pup so she could eat uninterrupted. Normally, the mother gave the pup clams that she had already opened, but once she gave the pup a closed clam and the pup pounded the clam on its chest and succeeded in opening it.

It quickly became obvious to us that the females with pups were spending more time feeding than the solitary otters. We hoped that the data collected at the automatic tracking station would tell us exactly how much more time females with pups spent feeding.

There were a lot more otters in Gibbon Anchorage compared to July and many of them were females with pups. It appeared that pups, which were now old enough to dive, had to learn to feed in shallow areas, so their mothers brought them into the anchorage. Females were freely swimming through different male territories.

Although the territorial boundaries seemed distinct, each bounded by a small cove or small islands, the territorial males changed frequently. A male would hang out in an area and suddenly one day he was gone and replaced by another male. We rarely saw any fights during the day, so we assumed that there must have been more male-male interactions at night.

Turk and I took turns doing the 5:00 AM net check. I never had any otters on my net-check days, so Turk got to sleep in. However, I always had to get up on Turk's days to check net because we frequently had otters to work up.

On September 14, at the 5:00 AM net check, we had a female and pup in one net and a twenty-seven-pound independent pup in the other. We worked up both pups without using drugs. The twenty-seven-pound pup chewed on the net in the boat as we were working on her and then she suddenly whirled around and tried to bite us. She actually nipped Turk's finger. After we placed a transmitter on her flipper she became even wilder and we could not obtain her body measurements. We knew she was only a pup by the color of the fur on her face and her bright white, sharp, unworn teeth.

The female woke up before receiving the antidote to the drug. She started thrashing around in the bow of the boat. We had two very active otters trying to bite us! We placed the pup next to its mother. The pup reached out and put its forepaws around her mother's neck, and the female did the same to the pup. It appeared like they were hugging each other. We gently nudged them out of the boat and they swam away together.

During feeding observations later in the day, we saw, for the first time, sea otters eating starfish (technically called sea stars). However, females with pups did not give any of the starfish to their young. We also saw a pup surface with rocks but no food.

The next evening there was a boat anchored in Log Cabin Bay. We drove up to see if everything was okay and they invited us aboard. There were three fishermen on the boat and they had fresh shrimp that they had just caught in their shrimp pots. They graciously served us a sautéed jumbo shrimp dinner. It was incredibly delicious. However, we stayed a little longer than we had anticipated. By the time we left it was dark and very foggy. Our boat had no lights and we did not have a flashlight. We could only occasionally glimpse a vague silhouette in the darkness that appeared to be the shoreline. We slowly headed toward Camp Cove, but had the misfortune of finding one of the submerged rocks just outside Log Cabin Bay. The motor clunked, but did not stall. As we looked behind the boat, we saw a yellowish-green glow in the water trailing from the motor. At first we thought something was leaking, but then realized it was the water, itself, glowing after being churned up by the prop. We remembered hearing about zooplankton that glowed when disturbed, but had not seen it before now. We decided to use it to our advantage. Turk grabbed a paddle and went to the side of the boat and repeatedly hit the water like a baseball bat, splashing it forward. This created a green glow of mist in the air, which enabled us to get our bearings as we putted along.

When we got back to the cabin we got a flashlight and looked at the prop. It had a little dent, but there was no serious damage.

Observations of otters became more and more interesting. We saw Duke try to interact with a female who had a large pup. The pup kept crawling on the female trying to nurse; this deterred Duke, who swam away from them. Fifteen minutes later Duke swam back to the female and bit her nose. The pup then bit Duke's nose! The pup then bit its mother's nose and she pushed it away with her forepaws. The pup decided to nurse and kept nursing as its mother groomed and rolled around in the water. It was rather hilarious to see the pup being flipped around each time the mother rolled. Duke gave up his courtship and swam away. The pup's strategy seemed to work, at least temporarily.

A half hour later we saw Duke with another female and pup feeding on mussels in less than one foot of water. Sometimes the pup got its own food, and sometimes it took food from Duke, but he did not retaliate.

We watched another female and pup feeding in Camp Cove. The pup squalled every time the female surfaced after a dive so she gave it some food. One time she gave the pup an empty clamshell just to get it to stop squalling!

A short distance from them, a big male was eating soft-shelled clams. Instead of opening the clams, he just popped the whole clam into his mouth. We could hear the crunching sounds from shore. We also saw him eat several of the fleshy, worm-like fat innkeepers. He would bite one end, and while holding the other end with his forepaws, pull back with his mouth until it burst. Then he slurped it up.

On September 17 a dense fog blanketed the anchorage. We worked close to the cabin all day because we were expecting the floatplane to arrive with our groceries and mail. Sometimes we thought we heard a plane overhead, but it never came. Did it bypass us because of the fog?

The next day we caught a male and female otter and a baby harbor seal together in one net. The harbor seal had a nose injury from being bitten by a sea otter. The wound appeared deep but it was not bleeding. A big harbor seal's head kept popping up around us as we worked to release the baby. It appeared to be its mother.

Although the weather was good, Chitina Air did not arrive again. We were starting to run low on food and were worried that they missed us on their mail run. We used the VHF radio to call the Cordova marine operator but no one answered. We did, however, reach the U.S. Fish and Wildlife Service in Anchorage and they called Chitina Air and found out that they had mechanical problems and planned to come out the next day.

September 19 was a beautiful, sunny, day but Chitina Air still did not arrive. At the first morning net check we caught a huge harbor seal. There was no way to get the seal disentangled in the water and it was so heavy it was almost impossible to get it on board the boat. However, after a considerable struggle we managed to do so. The seal, tangled in a chunk of net, thrashed around the bow of the boat. We put a heavier cargo net over its head to try to restrain it while we worked to free its flippers. When we had the seal nearly free he suddenly started thrashing again, and this time almost bit me. He also got even more tangled than he was originally. After an hour we finally freed it from the net; it took one and one-half hours to untangle the mess.

Chitina Air arrived the following day at noon, much to our relief, with food and mail. Part of our mail consisted of audiotapes from my family with family members talking to us. It was wonderful!

Each day we learned more about the otters. We watched a dispersed pup feed for an hour. It dove six times before surfacing with any food. It eventually pulled up some kelp and a starfish, which it nibbled but never ate, and then dove several more times before finding a crab. We were surprised at its low foraging success. How could it possibly find enough to sustain itself?

We continually monitored territorial males. They often left their areas during the day but always spent the night in their territories. Otto had come back to Camp Cove and he consistently followed this pattern, along with four other large males. The male that had temporarily replaced Otto in Camp Cove had left and was never seen again.

We were determined to catch Otto so we could find out where

he went when he left Camp Cove. We also wondered why these territorial males left their territories. Was there a better feeding area somewhere else? We placed two nets in Otto's territory but whenever we watched him he was wary of the net.

Several days later, as we walked on the beach, we saw Otto only five feet from shore. A female was hauled out on the beach near him in Camp Cove. When she saw us she quickly ran into the water and joined him. She left a fresh scat on the beach so we examined it and found mussel shells, limpets, and a few small clamshells. We watched them for hours and Otto stayed very close to her that evening.

At the net check the following morning we had a female and pup in one net in Camp Cove and another otter in the second net. We worked up the female and pup. The pup weighed sixteen pounds and was clearly far from being independent.

When we went to the second net we saw a large male with a nose scar. However, we were disappointed that the scar was on the opposite side of the nose as Otto's. We had planned for this to be the last day of trapping, so we resigned ourselves to not catching Otto. But how curious that there would be another male with a nose scar in Camp Cove, one that we've never seen before. It was not until we were about to drug him and he looked up at us that we came to the realization that our image of Otto's face was backwards. We had only been able to see his scar through the telescope, and the telescope reverses the image in the viewfinder, so we had visualized the scar on the wrong side of his nose. In fact, both of us had drawings of his nose in our field notes that were the reverse of reality. We had indeed caught Otto and we were ecstatic! Otto weighed seventy-three pounds. After we worked him up and released him, Big Brute, whose territory was at the mouth of Camp Cove and around the spit, swam into Camp Cove. Otto stayed in the back with a female and did not pay any attention to Brute. Brute finally swam out of the cove without incident, but we wondered if he sensed an opportunity to expand his territory when Otto was captured.

Trapping was finally over! What a nice way to end. We untangled the nets, pulled them into the boat one at a time, and lugged them into the shed. While we were working, a twenty-seven-foot sailboat came into Camp Cove. We went over to the boat and met an older couple with their son, on vacation from Fairbanks. We had coffee with them on their boat. They invited us to dinner that night so we brought slides of our research. After dinner there was a full moon so we could easily navigate our way back to the cabin.

The next day we noticed that the female in Camp Cove had a fresh scar on her nose. She must have bred with Otto during the night. We also found more fresh scats on the beach so we collected them and found the same food items that were in the last scat.

The family in the sailboat was still in Camp Cove so we drove them around the anchorage in our boat at low tide to show them the rocks. It was a very low tide so we used the opportunity to go clamming. That evening we joined the family in the sailboat for a glass of wine and invited them to dinner the next day in the cabin.

The following day Turk put a VHF antenna on a pole just outside the cabin and ran a cable to a receiver and discovered that we could hear the radio-signals of almost all of the otters from inside the cabin! We decided to move the automatic tracking station to the cabin. That would save a lot of time. We wouldn't have to walk ten minutes each way to check the station every day. Also, we could closely monitor the data recorded on the automatic tracking station to be sure it accurately depicted resting or feeding otters. We listened to the radio-signals on the receiver and watched the pens mark the recording paper. Initially, it seemed to be working better in the cabin than it did on the cliff. However, two days later we had to move it back because it was receiving very few signals. Apparently, it had been a fluke, maybe because all the otters happened to be close. Nevertheless, Otto's signal always came in strong in the cabin and we recalled Don's comment about being able to conduct our study from the kitchen table.

Otto spent the next day "tending" a female in the back of Camp Cove. Whenever she dove, he would dive, whenever she swam, he would swim beside her. However, the female was very thin, hauled out frequently, seldom foraged, and was sluggish whenever we approached her either from the boat or the beach, all of which indicated that she was sick. Once, when the female was hauled out, Otto grabbed her by the hind flippers and dragged her back into the water, overcoming her weak resistance. She snapped at him and then started swimming. He swam close beside her. Five minutes later he lunged on top of her back, grabbed her nose in his mouth, tumbled vigorously, and then they copulated for two and a half minutes before she was able to struggle away from him. The female hauled out five minutes later but got nervous when she detected us in the boat and returned to the water. Turk describes this incident as a rape in his thesis, the only one we observed during this study. Rapes (called forced copulations in the scientific literature) have been reported for several species of birds and mammals, but aside from this incident, have never been reported for sea otters.

The family from the sailboat came to dinner. We made clam chowder and spaghetti. I also made bread because we ran out of the fresh bread that we ordered with our groceries. It was always a challenge getting the dough to rise because it was quite cool in the cabin.

The weather was perpetually rainy, varying from a light mist to PAR. September 26 was so rainy and windy we could not radiotrack. We decided to take advantage of the very high tide that day to clean the underside of the boat. We drove the boat up onto two big logs on the beach, and after the tide went out, the boat was left high and dry. We scrubbed the underside to remove the accumulated algae and barnacles.

Although it rained every day, we could usually do some observations. We saw a female and pup resting sixty feet away from Brute in his territory by the end of the spit. While the mother rested, the pup licked her face. Brute swam slowly over to her, touched her gently, and then drifted away. The female followed very casually by sculling the water with her tail. Meanwhile, the pup was nursing. Brute quickly turned around and faced the mother, they vocalized, and then lightly bit each other's noses. The pup then bit Brute's nose and Brute swung one of his forepaws at the pup. Brute then nibbled at the female's crotch, while the pup put its forepaws around the female's neck, wedging its body between Brute and the mother. After interacting for ten minutes Brute swam off, appearing frustrated by the interfering pup. The female had acted as if she was receptive to breeding but was torn by her instincts to care for her pup.

Otto's territory had been vacant all day. We checked the automatic tracking station and found that he had left that morning. We went out in the boat and listened for his signal but could not find him. However, when we were radiotracking we discovered that a radio-transmittered female-pup pair had separated from each other. We located each of them in a different bay. When we reviewed the data from the automatic tracking station again, we saw that they had separated within the last two days. We also noticed that Duke was not recording at the station so we went to check his territory. As we peered into Southeast Bay with our binoculars, we saw a large white-headed otter swimming on his belly. "Oh no," we thought. "Duke's radio must have failed or come off." As the otter rolled onto its back we saw that it had no transmitter and no tags, so it wasn't Duke. How odd that another new otter would appear that we've never seen before. Watching awhile longer, the otter flared its flippers and we saw the signature holes of Big Brute. He wasted no time in taking over Duke's territory. The otters' territorial system was far more complex than we had imagined.

In Camp Cove the female that was raped by Otto was back. She was so thin we could see her ribs. She hauled out on the beach and then returned to the water and started feeding two feet from shore. She appeared to be eating something crunchy on the kelp. When she finished feeding we went to the area where she had been eating and pulled up some kelp. It had tiny mussels and snails on it. This seemed like a very poor diet for an adult otter. This otter left Camp Cove that night, and we did not see her again until we found her carcass on a nearby beach a few weeks later.

Two days later Otto was back in Camp Cove. Where had he been? We had hoped to find that out when we put a transmitter on him, but he obviously traveled beyond our search area, maybe to a better feeding spot. The weather had been horrendous so we guessed he had come back to seek the shelter of the cove. Did he know that even worse weather was on the way?

For the next ten days straight we had hard rain and gale winds.

In the middle of this stretch, one late afternoon, we were checking the automatic tracking station on the cliff and saw bright lights in the low dense clouds heading toward the anchorage. The visibility was so poor that we could not tell it was the *Montague* until it was right below us. What a day to make our gas delivery! We quickly ran back to the beach by the cabin and took the rowboat to the moored Boston Whaler and drove out to meet the *Montague.* Our boat bounced around in the whitecaps as the captain shouted some instructions to us. We couldn't hear him very well in the storm, but we saw him tie straps around each of two barrels, hoist them up in the winch, and then lower them into the water near our boat. We could not put them in the boat, as we were bouncing around too much, and it would have been too dangerous. We grabbed the straps, tied one barrel to each side of our boat, and slowly towed them to the beach by the cabin. The water was rough even in Camp Cove so getting the boat up to the beach without cracking the fiberglass bottom against the rocks was a challenge. We had to untie the barrels, float them to the edge of the water, and then roll them up the rocky beach. We had to repeat this procedure five times!

We wanted to give the captain some empty barrels to take back to Cordova because we had a $25 deposit on each barrel, but he was in a hurry and could not take them. That turned out to be okay with us because we were exhausted and soaked to the bone. Turk describes this briefly in his field notes, "*Montague* came today at 4:00 PM and brought us ten gas barrels." Maybe he was too tired to write any more.

When I went radiotracking the following day, I made a significant discovery about the range of the transmitters. Although most of the transmitters were very strong and could be heard from several miles away, I could not hear Otto's transmitter from just outside the anchorage. I knew he was still in Camp Cove because I had just seen him. That meant he did not necessarily travel as far away as we thought when he had disappeared for two days. I also discovered that his transmitter had drifted to a different frequency so it would not have recorded at the tracking station. Maybe when he left Camp Cove he was still quite close to the anchorage and not at some distant feeding area. It was nice to find this out, however, there was nothing we could do about it, and we wondered how many other transmitters were drifting to other frequencies. The technology of the transmitters and tracking station, the pioneering parts of this project, were frustratingly prone to problems.

After supper we sorted through the items in the shed to make room for the ten barrels of gas that were still standing at the high tide mark on the beach where we had left them. We then spent the next two hours rolling them into the shed and maneuvering them so they would fit. This was no easy task. By the time we finished my back was hurting and we were soaked with sweat. We decided to try a new way of washing up. Since it was raining so hard, we figured we would take a shower outside but have some pots of warm water to use to rinse off after we soaped up. It was quite invigorating, refreshing, and … "natural," standing naked in the rain, watching the eagles soar over, and watching Crazy Otto nonchalantly chomping clams in front of us.

On October 1 a boat anchored nearby. One of the passengers came to the cabin to say hi. He worked for the U.S. Fish and Wildlife Service in Anchorage and he and two others were on Green Island to hunt deer. We arranged to meet them the next day.

The following day we observed many different females with pups in several of the male territories. Did they come to breed, or just to seek the shelter of these protected coves, which "just so happened" to be male territories? One male followed a female and pup and frequently nuzzled at the female's groin. The pup squalled and kept trying to nurse, deterring the male's advances. One time the male pushed the pup off the female's nipple and the pup squalled even more loudly. The female responded by pushing away the male with her head. The male groomed momentarily and then tried to nuzzle the female's groin again. The female made a sharp cry and pushed him away again. He finally swam away (in disgust?).

We watched females with older pups feeding close together. We wondered if this was purposeful. The pups tumbled together and bit lightly on each other's heads. Sometimes a pup would try to get food from a female that was not its mother, although females never gave food to a pup that was not their own. We noticed that pups never stole food from each other.

We did observations from various vantage points in the anchorage, both on the shoreline and on the small islands. Each of the islands was unique in its own way. Island One was low, flat, and connected to the spit at very low tide. It was a good place to find otter-cracked clamshells. Island Two, which was across from the spit, had thick brush up to the shoreline so we never could find a place to do observations. Island Three, next to Island Two, was more rocky and open and we often chose it as an observation post. Island Four was our favorite place to do observations because it had a high, rocky cliff at one end overlooking a shallow shoal where females and pups liked to feed. Island Five had a nice view into Log Cabin Bay. It was covered with dense, herbaceous vegetation that we could not identify, but had a spectacularly nice aroma.

In the late afternoon we drove up to the boat in the anchorage with the deer hunters. We went aboard and had happy hour with the men. They did not have any success deer hunting. We decided to eat dinner together so they came to the cabin. They brought chili, steak, and liquor, and we supplied salad, bread, and dessert—obviously, we got the better deal. We had a great time with them. They agreed to take some empty gas barrels back to Cordova. When we went to the shed to get them, we were surprised to find that the rain had stopped and the sky was filled with brilliant stars.

Over the next several days we radiotracked and observed otters in each of the male territories. We were particularly interested in the mating success of each of the males—in other words, how many females did they each mate with. We wondered if there was any correlation between the size of the male, quality or size of his territory, and the number of mates. To gain this information we had to observe each male, multiple times per day. In order to do this, Turk and I split up and did observations from different sites in the anchorage and moved around frequently.

We had three beautiful days of sunshine, which made these observations that much more enjoyable. But then the rain started again. It was difficult to keep the telescope dry during the rain. We wrapped it in plastic bags, but if it was windy, rain would still blow onto the lens, blurring the image. Furthermore, the instructions that came with this very expensive telescope warned to never wipe the lens or it could become scratched. This instrument was made for watching stars on a clear night, not otters during a downpour. However, our study could not have been conducted without it.

On October 7, Turk was watching breeding activity in Southeast Bay while I was observing otters from the end of the spit. I saw a long copulation between Brute and a female previously tagged by Ancel. First, they were grooming beside each other and then they started to bite each other's nose and roll in the water. Then Brute climbed on top of the female's back. He bit her nose from behind, had his hind flippers around her body, his forepaws around her upper body and he thrusted. The female often whined like a pup as she rolled in the water. The copulation lasted thirty-five minutes. Afterwards, they swam together and each otter started grooming. The female licked her genital area and Brute groomed under his arms and on his chest. Then they rested very close together. The female frequently rested her head on Brute's arm, and then they would drift apart. Lying on their backs, they sculled with their tails to slowly move back together. One-half hour later they copulated again, and later in the afternoon I saw them mating again.

On October 9 we had our first snow. It was cold, but a nice change from the rain. By this time we had mapped out all the territories and also discerned a distinct pattern in the mating behavior. Most females stayed with a male in his territory for two days. Males actively kept prospective mates from leaving. Typically, on day one they mated several times. On the second day, the female and male groomed, fed, and rested close together, but did not copulate. On the third day, the female left the territory. Males frequently bred with a different female the day after his previous mate left his territory. However, males did not breed with more than one female at a time. Because of this, some males may not have been available to breed when certain females came into estrus.

We wondered how much choice females had in the selection of their mate. We saw some females come into Otto's territory; they tumbled and nuzzled with him, but then left the area. Did they see him as unfit and purposely reject him, or were they just not ready to breed at that time? Otto was quite a bit smaller than both Duke and Brute. He was also not as white-headed as the two of them. The white-headedness, particularly when the fur was dry, gave the otters a distinguished, regal, appearance. If we could see these differences, then certainly the female otters did, as well. They must have also picked up on subtle behavioral cues that we did not recognize. It did seem to us that, in very anthropomorphic terms, Brute had a particularly suave manner with the ladies (more of a charmer compared to Otto's aggressive style). Brute's territory was also in a much better location than Otto's. Brute's was on the main travel route in and out of the north end of the anchorage. It also encompassed the best feeding spot for Helmet crabs. In contrast, to enter Otto's territory, a female would have to pass all the way through Brute's territory.

Specific to this time of year, we began to see several otters in the anchorage haul out of the water onto the beach. One male sniffed along the shore and then walked up the beach thirty yards sniffing the whole way. After a few minutes he hobbled back down to the water. He was obviously looking (smelling) for something. Had an estrus female been up that beach?

One afternoon we walked along the beach and saw a tagged pup that had separated from her mother, hauled out on the beach. We got within five feet of her and took lots of pictures. Her transmitter had already come off. She ran into the water and left a scat on the beach, which was all mussels. This fit with our observations that pups frequently fed on mussels. Mussels can be plucked off rocks in shallow water and are highly visible even to a human observer. Clams, which are buried three-to six-inches in the sediment, and are in deeper water, obviously require much more skill to find and dig up. Also, otters simply pop the whole mussel in their mouth and eat it, shell and all, whereas most clams have harder shells and are generally shucked before consuming the meat.

A few days later we walked within ten feet of a female and pup hauled out on the beach. It appeared that females and females with pups hauled out frequently, but males only hauled out if they were with a female or looking for a female. When otters were hauled out they were usually a few yards from the water's edge.

They occasionally went up as far as the grass above the high tide mark, but rarely ventured further up into the shrubs or trees at the edge of the forest. In contrast, river otters traveled well up into the forest.

On October 22 we made another discovery regarding mating behavior. We were driving the boat to the spit to do observations and saw Brute fifteen feet from shore and a female halfway between him and the shore. After we landed the boat on the beach we heard a pup squalling in the grass, approximately thirty feet from the edge of the water. We slowly and quietly walked toward the squalling pup. Suddenly, a large pup bolted out of the grass and we had to move out of its way as it awkwardly hobbled down to the water. It entered the water about one hundred feet from the mother, but because the water was so rough, they did not see each other. Also, the wind was very strong and the mother could not hear her pup squalling. In fact, the mother and Brute dove and swam off in different directions, apparently bothered by our presence. The pup seemed panicked as it periscoped looking for its mother and swam around in circles, squalling. Then it hauled out of the water and looked toward the grass. We interpreted this to mean that it had last been with its mother up in the grass, and maybe it had fallen asleep and she left it there. When it did not see its mother, it returned to the water and continued to swim and yell loudly.

Five minutes later, Brute swam close to shore and kept looking up at the grass as if he were looking for the female. After another ten minutes, the female suddenly appeared, found her pup, and with hardly a greeting, they started feeding together. We had been concerned that our appearance at this inopportune time might have prematurely caused the split of this female and her pup, and were relieved to see that it hadn't.

At the beginning of the breeding season we thought a female would only breed after separating from its pup, and that family breakup might even be caused by the courtship behavior between the male and female. Now, several observations indicated that breeding could occur even in the presence of the pup. We had seen some females with fresh nose scars still attended by their pups. And now today, it appeared that the female had hauled out with her pup and then snuck back into the water to breed when her pup was sleeping. Two human intruders unfortunately foiled this plan.

As we saw more and more interactions between territorial males and females with pups, it became apparent that the courtship process was much more extended than between males and lone females. Females with pups seemed torn between their maternal instincts and their desire to breed. Males seemed persistent, but patient, often tending a female and pup pair for several days. Even after this period of time, they would not necessarily be successful at mating.

Although each day we continued to learn a little bit more about the private lives of sea otters, our observations became more and more difficult. Day length was rapidly shortening. It was now dark from 6:00 PM to 7:00 AM. The rain and wind were relentless, and it was becoming cold. Driving the boat in the cold pelting rain became like a torture treatment. The person not driving would typically sit on the wooden bench seat facing backwards, hood up, and basically unaware of what was ahead. We wore orange rubber fishermen's gloves to keep our hands from getting too numb. We were constantly frustrated by the continually fogging binoculars. We kept them inside our raincoats but they fogged or got splattered with raindrops seconds after we pulled them out to make an observation. Despite these difficult conditions, we continued to enjoy the wildlife all around us. Every day we saw small flocks of harlequin ducks and surf scoters bobbing along close to shore, and oystercatchers yakking away at the spit. We were also monitoring a pair of bald eagles in the back of Camp Cove.

The rain made us rely more and more on Ancel's blind. Turk began doing several all-night tracking sessions from there. We clamped an antenna to a thirty-foot metal pole and lashed it to the blind. From inside the blind we could swivel the pole to direct the antenna to the strongest signal and listen for the otters' activity. Turk was not satisfied with the operation of the automatic tracking station so he wanted to get more activity data by listening to the signals through the night when the otters were most active. The blind, however, was getting saturated from the persistent rain. To prepare for an all-night tracking session, Turk would line the inside of the blind with plastic. To stay warm, he curled up inside a sleeping bag—curl here is quite literal because the blind was so small you could not stretch out. As it got colder and darker, he resorted to bringing the Coleman lantern into the blind with him. He claimed he did this in order to read, but in truth, I think it was to stay warm. Every half hour he would scan through all the frequencies of the otters and listen for several minutes on each one to determine their activity. In the morning, I would take his place and continue activity monitoring through the daylight hours, using both visual observations and telemetry. In this way, we could collect twenty-four hours of continuous data for several days in a row.

One very stormy day, we sat in the cabin and started compiling the data. We had captured and transmittered eighteen otters at Green Island, but were presently monitoring only half of them. Some otters had left the area. Others had pulled off their transmitters after only one of the two attachment bolts corroded causing the transmitter to flop around on the flipper. Turk hadn't counted on this when he did his corrosion experiments in the aquarium back in Minnesota. The other technology that worked in the lab but not in the field was the transmitters themselves—we found that several had malfunctioned. The malfunctioning transmitters were particularly frustrating because the only way to detect them was to search around and look at every otter's flippers to see if we could identify individuals whose signal we could not hear. This used up an enormous amount of time.

By the end of October we were more than ready to leave Green Island. It rained twenty-five of the last thirty days. In fact, Turk described the weather as "downright raunchy" in his field notes. It was cold on most days and the water temperature was thirty-eight degrees. Our rain gear was ripped all over and we got soaked every time we went outside. We spent our last day cleaning the cabin and packing. We received a northwind October 24 stating that the plane would arrive the next morning at 10:30 AM to pick us up. Ancel was flying out to Green Island and we would leave on the same floatplane. We were worried that the plane would not come because it was raining hard and the winds were howling at 70–80 mph, churning the water in the anchorage to a frothy white.

Female and pup in net

Otter hauled out on land

# The End of Our First Field Season

We were amazed the next morning when we woke up to sunshine. We carried all of our gear down to the beach. Since it was such a clear, calm, day, we took the opportunity to snap some last photos of Otto cruising around his territory, looking inquisitively at us. The sunshine on his white head made for some spectacular shots. We had become so attached to him that we found ourselves talking to him and imagining that he was listening. We told him we hoped the winter wouldn't be too harsh, and we'd see him next year.

Chitina Air arrived at 10:30 AM and Ancel and another researcher got off the plane. We wished we had time to talk to Ancel about our many interesting observations, but because we were leaving and the pilot was in a rush, we only had time to mention a few quick things while we all hurriedly packed the plane. The pilot had several flights to do that day because he had been weathered out the previous three days. He told us there was no time to radiotrack to locate some of the otters that were missing, but we managed to convince him to make a few passes over Orca Inlet and Nelson Bay so we could count the otters there.

When we got out of the plane in town we noticed that our camera was nowhere to be found. We realized that it must have been left on the beach at Green Island; apparently no one saw it sitting there as four of us quickly packed the plane. The pilot from

Chitina Air had to fly back to that part of the sound and said he would stop at Green Island to pick up the camera. However, we knew that the tide was coming in and worried that it would soon wash over the camera. We tried to coax the pilot to leave right away, but he insisted on having a leisurely cup of coffee. Whether it was that cup of coffee that doomed the camera, we will never know. By the time he got back to Green Island it was already submerged underwater and no one could find it. Later that day, at low tide, Ancel found the camera, but it was too late. We lost a lot of great pictures—the last ones of Otto.

After doing errands that afternoon we went to the Reluctant Fisherman coffee shop for dinner. Although we were celebrating the end of the field season, the Reluctant Fisherman restaurant was too far above our means. We met a crewmember from the *Enforcer* and he took us to a bar that had a live band so we could continue our celebration. He introduced us to many other people who kept buying us drinks. We did not get back to our trailer until 3:30 in the morning and we definitely drank too much! As was typical, Turk understates this in his field notes—"We met a guy from the *Enforcer* and had a few beers with him."

Over the next two days we did errands and packed. We stopped by the Fish and Game office to meet with people, report our findings, and thank them for all the assistance they had given to us. Dick and Kay Groff had us over for dinner and wanted to hear about all the adventures of the "otter spotters." It seemed almost strange to sit in a warm, dry, house with comfortable furniture. On October 28 we locked up our trailer and left Cordova in the rain. Our first field season was over!

We were pleased with all that we had accomplished. However, there were several methodological issues regarding the tracking station and transmitters that had to be improved for the next season. We had answered some key questions that also generated a host of new ones. We had survived several harrowing experiences and wondered if the worst of these was behind us.

# Season Two Begins

Turk went to Alaska twice during the winter and collected data in northeast Prince William Sound and on Green Island. He saw large groups of otters in Orca Inlet and much smaller groups in Nelson and Simpson Bays, which demonstrated that otters move seasonally. We were later able to show that some of these seasonal movements were caused by boat traffic, namely, the opening and closing of the various commercial fisheries.

On Green Island, two of the territorial males were gone, but our favorites, Brute and Otto, remained. Males still attempted to court females by tending them, but Turk did not see any copulations. There were several young bucks in the anchorage filling in some of the vacant territories, but they were destined to be short-timers.

Turk also saw two females with very small, fuzzy pups in December, which meant they were born in November. Generally, females give birth in the spring so the bulk of pup rearing occurs when the weather is more favorable. Being born at the start of the winter, when it is cold, stormy, and dark most of the day, seems like a cruel joke.

In early May 1981, Turk went to Green Island with one of Ancel's field assistants, Jerry. I had to work in Minneapolis until mid-May in order to receive a six-month leave of absence from my job. On May 19 I flew to Cordova, did errands in town, and then flew to Green Island on a floatplane. Jerry flew back to Cordova.

The next day, eleven of the twenty-one otters that we observed had tags on their flippers. We were glad to see that so many had made it through the winter, which is a time of high mortality. Unfortunately, several of the transmitters and even some of the flipper tags were missing. Only one large male was in the same territory as last fall, yet he was not in Gibbon Anchorage during the winter. We wondered where he had been, and we also wanted to know where Brute and Otto were because they were nowhere to be found.

There were a lot of females with pups in the anchorage. Some of the pups were very small and looked like little "fuzz-balls." We watched their mothers teach them to swim. A mother would swim twenty feet away and then wait for her pup to come to her. At this young age, the pup would swim on its stomach and paddle hard to get to its mother. A few other pups were larger and swam without difficulty.

We noticed that three to five females rested together and did not interact with each other. They did not appear to be as social as the males in Nelson Bay.

Males, however, frequently swam up to females and interacted with them. They often returned to the same female over and over again and hugged, sniffed, and tumbled with her. This couldn't merely have been to determine whether the female was in estrus. The male would have known this after the first interaction. We wondered why they had these pre-breeding interactions. Was it to gain familiarity—like human dating? Or, did the interactions themselves prompt the female to come into estrus? We even saw some copulations, but they were all much shorter than the ones we observed in the fall. In one case, the copulation lasted only ten seconds because the female broke away and swam off.

We went clamming at low tide, eager to resurrect the clam chowder recipe that we had perfected the previous fall. We knew of an area that was good for soft-shelled clams. We found that the highest density of clams was in a band somewhat higher up on the beach than the lowest tide level. We saw two types of holes in the mud and learned that the circular holes were from fat innkeepers, and the elongated holes were from soft-shelled clams. The clam, buried in the mud, poked its long siphon up through the sediment to the water, from which it extracted minute food particles. When the tide was out, and it could no longer filter-feed, it withdrew its siphon, leaving the characteristic hole. When we pushed the shovel too close to an elongated hole and started to pry upward, the shell frequently broke from the pressure of the mud. We learned to dig eight inches away from the hole, carefully lift the mud, and gently remove the clams with our hands. These clams were three inches in diameter—a good size for us, as well as the otters.

Within a few days of arriving on Green Island, I developed a raised, bumpy, rash on my left arm. Two days later it spread to my right arm and itched fiercely. I could not figure out what caused it. This was my welcome back to Alaska—something new, unknown, unanticipated, and likely to get worse before it got better.

Since the weather was better than in the fall, we did more exploratory trips to places outside the anchorage. One day, we drove to Little Green Island (fig. 3) and saw a group of otters resting in a kelp bed (seaweed). They used the kelp as an anchor. They draped fronds of kelp over their body so they could sleep without drifting away. This type of kelp, called *Nereocystis*, had very long strands with a round bulb on one end that floated on the surface. When looking from a distance, each of these bulbs looked like the head of an otter, so at first glance there appeared to be fifty or sixty otters, when in reality, there were about a dozen. As we got closer to the group, we noticed that several of them were interacting; much more like the males in Nelson Bay than the females we had seen in and around the anchorage. We wondered if this might be a small, isolated, male area and could be one of the places that the territorial males went when they left Gibbon Anchorage. There were no pups in this group and there were several big white-headed otters. Unfortunately, we did not see Brute or Otto.

We planned to leave Green Island at the end of May to return to Nelson Bay. We had obtained a lot of information on the number of otters using the anchorage, how many of these were females with pups, how many were lone females, and how many were males. We knew which territorial males were back from last year and which ones were missing. We also had conducted several counts of otters all around Green Island so we could monitor changes in numbers and distribution on a larger scale than just in the area in and around the anchorage. We were lucky that the weather was good, which made data collection much easier. On the other hand, the otters also seemed to take advantage of the sunny weather and calmer seas. Instead of crowding into the protected nooks and crannies of the anchorage, they were dispersed well off shore. That made it harder for us to collect feeding data because there were fewer animals around to observe.

The time was right to see what was happening in the northeastern part of the sound. Besides, my rash was intolerable and I needed to seek some medical care. I wondered if there might be a local Alaskan remedy, analogous to soaking the worm-infested blueberries in salt water.

Figure 3. Green Island, Channel Island, and Little Green Island.

# A Swim, a Storm, and a Setback

On May 28 we cleaned the cabin and packed up the boat to drive to Cordova. We left Green Island at noon. The water in the anchorage was choppy, and as we rounded the bend outside the anchorage, it was even rougher, with whitecaps as far as we could see. We figured we would just take it easy and slowly plow forward through the oncoming waves. We told ourselves that this year we weren't going to do anything stupid.

Just fifteen minutes into the trip we hit a deep trough between waves and suddenly heard a splash behind us. We jerked the throttle back and looked to see whether something was following us. It took a moment to realize that it was not a whale, porpoise, or seal, but it was our motor. The 25-hp spare motor was gone. We ran to the back, looked over, and saw it submerged, dangling from the safety line that was attached to the boat. With neither of us at the controls, the boat was getting buffeted by the waves and had spun around in the other direction so that the waves were washing over the stern. There was barely enough room for the two of us to stand in the back corner of the boat because the big motor took so much room. And there was nothing to grab to keep from getting washed out while bending over trying to hoist up the dead weight of the submerged motor. We were also worried that as the motor twisted around underwater the line would break and we would lose it. Or, just as bad, that it would hit and crack the lower unit of the main motor and damage it. We didn't want to have to call the Coast Guard again, especially so early in the season.

Somehow we managed to muscle the motor to the surface and then into the boat. Shaken by this experience, and now without a usable spare motor, we decided to head back to the cabin. We probably would not have made this decision last year, but we prided ourselves for being somewhat wiser and more cautious this year.

Back at the cabin, we waited, hoping the water would calm down, but by late afternoon we realized we would have to stay on Green Island for the night. We unpacked some of the gear and cooked supper. After dinner we made chocolate pudding and set it on the counter to cool while we went outside to reset the mooring for the boat. Unexpectedly, the water was flat calm. I said, "Let's go now!" Turk, though, who seemed fixed on the dessert that we just made, said, "But the pudding!" I said, "Grab the pot and two spoons and let's get out of here!"

We quickly repacked the boat, grabbed the pot of pudding, and closed up the cabin. We were on our way at 8:00 PM in a light rain with the pudding on the console.

As we hit the ocean entrance an hour later, the waves were building and daylight was fading. We started questioning whether we really had become any wiser in our decisions. Fortunately, the water calmed down and it quit raining so we had smooth sailing into Cordova. The last hour of the trip was in the dark, but we could see the landforms and the water clear enough to navigate without a problem. We pulled up to the dock in Cordova at 10:30 PM.

The first priority the following day was to deal with my rash. Red, raised, bumps had spread all over my legs, arms, chest, and back. They itched a lot. I went to the medical clinic and the doctor did not know what caused it, but gave me some medication. It gradually improved over the next ten days. I hoped I was not allergic to something at Green Island that I would encounter again when we went back.

In the meantime, Turk worked on the trailer. He got the refrigerator going but the heater and toilet did not work—déjà vu from last year! One might not think that a heater would be necessary in June, but it really did make the difference between being comfortable and being miserable. Throughout the summer we wore thermal underwear and wool clothes under our rain gear to shield off the chilly dampness. Coming back to a cold, damp, cramped, dimly lit trailer after a full day's work on the water was going to make me long for the tent camp and the bears at Nelson Bay. At least we had a kerosene heater in the tent. We did not look forward to the prospect of hanging up our wet clothes in the evening and getting up the next morning at the crack of dawn, with the temperature in the forties, and putting on the same, cold, soggy clothes.

We looked forward to going to the post office and picking up our mail. I was happy to see a letter from my mother. She wrote that my father was not feeling well and was going to have tests on his colon. She provided no other information, but it nagged at me.

The next day we went to the outboard motor shop to seek their advice about the motor that had fallen in the salt water. Several of the guys in the shop recognized us and wanted to know about the sea otters. Fortunately, they told us that the motor was probably not ruined and explained what we could do to get it running again. We worked on it that afternoon and got it started. Next, we went to the hardware store where they gave us some parts and tips for fixing the heater in the trailer. In order to work on the heater one had to be a bit of a contortionist. Turk had his head on the floor and his legs outside the door of the trailer in the rain. After replacing the part, he lit a match and the pilot started. One full minute later, he turned the knob to the heat position and we cheered at hearing the "whoosh" of the burner. "Second major accomplishment of the day!" he said with satisfaction. The day was topped off when our good friend, Dick Groff, came to visit us in a warm trailer.

The next day I called home and was happy to hear that my father was diagnosed with diverticulitis, an infection in his colon. I was quite relieved because I was so worried that he had cancer.

We then took the boat to the Olsen Bay warehouse to get supplies for camp. We were smart this year and brought ski goggles to wear in the boat to keep the rain from pelting our eyes. We also brought a case of large plastic bags from Minnesota to stow our gear in so it wouldn't get wet in the boat or at camp. Turk had searched hard for bags that were made of heavy-duty plastic, and the only ones he could find were bright red. So this became the field season of red plastic. We did not overload the bow of the boat this time and handled the five-foot waves without difficulty. We went to Nelson Bay and set up the tent and boat mooring in the rain.

Don came the next day so we all stayed at camp. After unpacking, we set up a target and practiced shooting the rifle, anticipating that the bears would be back. I hit the target two out of five shots, still not a great record. I hoped it would not come back to haunt me.

On June 3 we went back to the Olsen Bay warehouse to get nets for trapping and other supplies. The water was surprisingly calm around Point Gravina. For several minutes three killer whales swam parallel to us, one hundred feet away. Their large triangular dorsal fin sliced through the water and we could easily hear them breathing. On our way back Don suggested that we stop at his favorite "hot spot" in Sheep Bay to fish. We caught four rockfish for dinner.

We went to Simpson Bay the next day to walk the beach and look for remains of otters that had died over the winter. One person stayed in the boat while the other two walked along the storm-tide line—the very highest water level mark on the beach where floating debris accumulates. I was in the boat radiotracking while Don and Turk were on the beach walking toward each other. This time we were careful to designate a meeting spot so we wouldn't experience the same fiasco as last year in Sheep Bay.

We only had one rifle, which Turk was carrying, so of course, it was Don that first encountered the bear. He had the sense that something was following him. He stopped, looked back, and saw a three hundred-pound black bear approaching him. He stood still and yelled at the bear. Just then, Turk arrived from the other direction and the two of them yelled loudly and threw rocks toward the bear. The bear veered off his path and meandered into the woods. A minute later, though, it reappeared on the beach. The bear's head was down and he acted as if he was looking for something on the beach and was unaware of Turk and Don, but, in fact, was walking straight at them. Again, they threw rocks and, again, the bear veered off toward the woods. The bear then reappeared and began to walk along the grassy berm that marked the storm-tide line, exactly where Turk and Don were standing. Turk and Don moved down the beach toward the edge of the water to allow the bear to pass by, but the bear followed them, curiously acting as though it wasn't after them per se, but just happened to want to go exactly where they went. Turk then called me on the walkie-talkie and said they needed an immediate pick up. They chased the bear away one more time with rocks, but it was only momentarily deterred and followed them down toward the water. When I roared up in the boat the bear finally ran off as Turk and Don jumped in.

The next day we went to Cordova and picked up Jerry (Ancel's assistant) and the veterinarian from California who had supplied us with the immobilizing drugs. When we got back to camp we set out one capture net. We were excited to test some modifications of the transmitters and tags that Turk had devised over the winter. For the transmitters, he made a new attachment that we hoped would not come off the flipper as easily. He also mounted one transmitter on a collar made of surgical tubing to see if it would stay on an otter's neck. For the tags, we were going to use a small screw to keep the otters from prying open the distal end and removing them from their flippers.

The next morning at 4:00 AM we had four otters in the net. It took over four hours to work them up. We decided to try the experimental collar on one of them along with a flipper transmitter. Turk spent twenty minutes adjusting the collar to fit the neck of the otter so it was not too tight or too loose. When the otter woke up after it was given Narcan, it dove into the water from the bow of the boat. It surfaced fifteen feet from the boat, turned around, and faced us. It grabbed the collar with its forepaws, slipped it over its head, and dropped it in the water. Then it turned around and dove away. We laughed so hard we doubled over in the boat. "I hope you weren't counting on collaring anymore otters," I teased Turk.

We untangled the net later in the day, and in the early evening we caught another four otters. The following morning we caught two more otters and a mother and baby harbor seal. It was a good thing we only had one net in the water. We were in high spirits even though it was pouring all day.

In the late afternoon we went down to the boat to do the net check, but could not pull the boat to shore. The long loop of rope onto which the boat was attached, which ran from the mooring to shore, was stuck at the O ring on the buoy. The five of us pulled as hard as we could but the rope would not budge. Don suggested that we use the rifle to try to shoot the buoy, but we all rejected that because we had visions of putting a hole in Ancel's boat! Ultimately, we decided that someone would have to swim out there and see what was wrong. Jerry volunteered, indicating that he swam laps at the YMCA in Anchorage. We started to discuss it, but before we knew it, he stripped off all his clothes and jumped into the forty-eight-degree water! He stroked hard initially, but faded quickly as the cold made him gasp for air. With our encouraging shouts from shore, he made it to the boat and struggled to climb in. He found that the buoy had twisted twelve times around the rope. Jerry leaned over the bow, untwisted the line, and then unhooked the boat so he could pick us up on shore. However, that turned out to be a mistake. He had trouble starting the engine and the strong wind that had caused the problem in the first place was blowing him out into Nelson Bay. All I could see was Jerry's bare body bent over the steering wheel frantically trying to get the boat started. He had never driven the boat so he didn't know the little tricks that we used to start it. We were all yelling instructions to him from shore, but our voices were lost in the strong wind. In just a few minutes he had drifted completely out of our sight in the dense fog. Suddenly, we heard the motor start and he came back into view and landed on the beach. We were all laughing hysterically, but then realized that Jerry was shivering and blue so we rushed him up to the tent. He dried off and huddled over the kerosene heater as we made him hot chocolate. When we finally got out to the net, we had caught five otters, including one that was blind in one eye (not related to the capture). While we were processing these otters, another one swam into the net and got caught, seemingly attracted to others, despite our presence.

Two days later we caught eight otters in the net at once. We had to let three of them go without working them up because they would have put us over the limit of our permits. Trapping was over in only four days.

We radiotracked, walked beach in Sheep and Nelson Bays, checked the automatic tracking station, and conducted feeding observations until June 12. Then we took Don and Jerry to Cordova to catch their plane. The veterinarian had left earlier in the week. Before Don and Jerry left, we had three days in a row of sunshine and sixty degrees. It was a good time to practice using the dart gun that the veterinarian had left for us. Obviously, we did not need it in Nelson Bay, but it might be helpful for targeting specific otters at Green Island. The gun worked by pumping it up to a certain air pressure, which could be adjusted depending upon the length of the shot. It shot a light plastic dart that held the tranquilizing drugs. The good thing about the dart was that it was so light in weight it would have a low impact and not harm the otters. The bad thing, though, was that a small breeze could blow it off its mark.

We wanted to concentrate more on feeding observations. On one level, watching feeding otters through a telescope was always intriguing. On the other hand, the tenacious black flies really tested our patience. We wore gloves and netted bug hats. We would try to attach the netting to the eyepiece of the telescope to seal out the bugs, but they always seemed to find a way in. Sitting still, not taking your eye away from the telescope for at least thirty minutes, was quite a challenge.

We noticed that otters were not eating many crabs this year. Did they cause the population to crash in just one year?

We also made several other interesting observations. We saw, for the first time, a female and pup in Nelson Bay. She did not rest in the raft with all the males. We also saw one tagged otter that we had captured on Green Island. We were amazed to learn that otters swam from Green Island to Nelson Bay (over sixty miles). We also noticed that the signals from the transmitters were weaker than last year, and some transmitters failed to work at all. We saw the transmitters on the otters and the antennas were normal, just no signal was coming from them. We were only able to locate fifteen of the twenty-one otters that we had just transmittered.

We were worried that the weaker signal of the transmitters would not be received by the automatic tracking station. Therefore, we compared the data recorded on the strip chart paper to the data we collected while radiotracking. We were pleased to find that it was recording properly, although we learned that the tracking station was picking up static on one otter's frequency.

Every evening when we checked the tracking station we saw a harbor seal splashing around just beyond the boat mooring. We wondered if it was the same one as last year.

On June 17 we decided to radiotrack all night because it seemed like the weather would be good. We watched rafts of resting otters become smaller and smaller during the evening until all otters were feeding at 1:30 AM. We set up the boat bed and tarp and I took the first shift in the sleeping bag while Turk radiotracked. We agreed that he would not do any quick starts to chase down an otter. We were in a good position in the middle of the bay to hear many of the otters, so Turk dropped the anchor. Turk saw lights in the distance over the silhouette of the mountain peaks. On many other occasions we had seen northern lights so he did not bother to wake me up because he did not think it was that spectacular.

Northern lights typically get bright, then dim, disappear, and then reappear. That is exactly what was happening. The only odd thing that Turk noticed was that overhead the sky was starless, whereas northern lights almost always occurred in a clear sky. Just as he was pondering this, it started raining and getting very windy. Suddenly there was a bright flash and a jolting roll of thunder, followed by two more in quick succession. This was obviously no northern lights. This was our first thunderstorm in Alaska!

Turk immediately took down the antenna, which was mounted on a ten-foot pole, and then rushed to the bow to pull up the anchor. Meanwhile, I had jumped out of the sleeping bag and was trying to get on my hip boots, float coat, and rain gear. Turk was very tired and the anchor was firmly lodged in the muck. He was having a hard time pulling it up. Suddenly, another blast of lightening came very close to the boat. Panic stricken, and not yet fully dressed, I rushed to the front and grabbed the anchor line. With my adrenalin rushing, the anchor was on board before we knew it. We momentarily debated heading toward camp but then elected to head to the closest shore instead (probably a good decision). Once we got to shore, we got out of the boat and sat by some rock cliffs until the storm passed an hour later. It was quite impressive how much rain and lightening occurred during that hour. But then it all stopped as suddenly as it had appeared. At 4:00 AM we got back in the boat and bilged out six inches of water. We resumed radiotracking and by the time we were finished, the sun was out. We went back to camp to grab the telescope because we wanted to watch the morning raft formation.

At 4:45 AM there were two otters resting together near the center of the bay, the seed for the eventual raft. Then otters started swimming toward them from all directions. By 7:15 AM there was one raft of forty otters near another raft of ten otters. We saw the female and pup and realized that the female was Kate, whom we had caught last year in Nelson Bay. She never joined the raft. Three males followed her. They grabbed her nose and sniffed her groin. She left her pup floating on the surface and then dove at the males to chase them off. The hassle of being the only female in an all male area was obvious, and probably the reason that other females stayed away. Given that otters knew their way around a large area of the sound, we wondered why Kate would put up with this. Maybe she did, in fact, like all of the attention.

We went back to camp at 8:30 AM, had breakfast, and hit the sack. After sleeping eight hours, we drove to Cordova to treat ourselves to a movie, only to be disappointed to find out that the movie only ran on Monday and Thursday nights. We decided to stay in the trailer that night.

Over the next few weeks we did a lot more observations of the morning raft formation. We learned that in Nelson Bay they typically formed one massive raft of over one hundred otters. After resting for several hours, that raft fractured into smaller ones. Some otters frequently swam from one raft to another. Then most of them split off to feed by themselves for one to three hours, after which they joined a smaller raft later in the day.

Over the course of these observations we saw several otters that we had tagged and transmittered either this year or last year.

All of last year's otters had lost their transmitters and only had flipper tags remaining. These individuals could be identified by the different tag colors and positions on their flippers.

We were disheartened to learn, though, that half of the newly attached transmitters had failed. We saw the otters with binoculars or through the telescope but could not hear their radio-signals. It was so discouraging to have worked so hard trapping, and to have spent so much effort over the winter designing a better attachment mechanism, only to have another technical problem that was beyond our control. We decided to test the transmitters planned for use on Green Island by putting them in salt water for a week. If any failed, we would send them back to the company for replacement.

One day we took a trip to observe the otters in Simpson Bay and saw a group of seventeen otters feeding close together. This was very unusual. Normally they fed alone. Even more surprising, they were all eating kelp. We had seen a few young otters at Green Island eating mussels and snails attached to kelp, but never the kelp itself. Here, they were actually devouring the kelp and appeared to be relishing it. In fact, some otters stole kelp from others. There was also a flock of thirty glaucous-wing gulls swarming around them, some sitting in the water and others circling overhead. One very bold gull even landed on an otter's chest and stole the kelp. A second bold gull landed on an otter and the otter swat at it with its forepaws, and then rolled over to keep the gull from being able to take the kelp.

There was obviously something very special about this kelp and we needed to find out what it was. We attempted to dredge some up using the anchor. After five unsuccessful attempts, we devised a different plan. We decided to try to steal a piece of kelp from an otter. We rushed toward an otter in the boat, hoping that it would dive and leave the kelp on the surface. In the first attempt, however, the otter clutched onto the valuable kelp when it dove. In the second attempt, the otter did leave the kelp on the surface, but a gull quickly snatched it up and flew off. He landed in the water thirty feet from us. We immediately sped toward him and he flew off leaving the kelp on the surface. As the kelp was sinking, we grabbed it from the water. The kelp had lots of small, white, round, herring eggs on it—a valuable treat indeed! We measured the depth of the water in this spot and it was over 120 feet deep.

As days went on we took advantage of some very low tides and dug for clams. We frequently made clam chowder and steamed clams for dinner. We joked about becoming like the otters.

We frequently saw fishing boats in the various bays and noticed that some of them purposely drove toward rafts of otters to break them up. We mentioned this to Al, the shellfish biologist at the Alaska Department of Fish and Game, and he told us that a number of fishermen were getting very frustrated by the otters. In fact, he told us a story of a drunken man who drove a boat to the area where otters were hauled out on the mud and shot several of them. A woman saw him do it, but was afraid to accost him, and he was never caught. Al had heard of several other cases of people who had shot otters during the winter. People had clearly connected the demise of the Dungeness crab fishery to the otters. This may have explained why our counts of sea otters were about one hundred less than last year.

The next day I heard six gunshots across Nelson Bay as I was doing observations. Every time there was a shot the otters startled in the raft and dove. At about the same time, Turk was trying to count otters in a large raft, and a boat came by and plowed right through the center. Turk drove up to the boat and said to a man, "I've been out here several hours studying the rafts and when you drive through them it ruins my study." The man responded nervously, "Oh, you're the sea otter guy. Sorry, I just wanted the kids to be able to take pictures." Then one of the kids asked Turk, "Do you shoot otters?" The man quickly said, "No, no." We realized that we needed to investigate any shots that we heard in order to report any potential poachers. Attitudes had certainly changed since last year.

We noticed that the otters were also much more skittish of our boat. We were unable to drift close to a raft. We figured it was probably due to the increased and intentional disturbance by the fishermen. Behaviors had changed on both sides.

We were settling into camp life at Nelson Bay and were enjoying it because it was just the two of us, and so far, no bears. However, we frequently had other smaller visitors. There seemed to be an invasion of shrews in our tent. We found a dead one in the pancake mix and another determined shrew kept trying to climb into a basin full of dirty dishes. Turk caught it by the tail and threw it into the stream. We set mousetraps and caught eight shrews in five days.

When we awoke on June 29 it was freezing cold in the tent. We looked outside and saw that the mountains were covered in snow. It was hard to believe it was summer.

Later in the day we saw a boat anchored near the end of the stream by camp. A few hours later, at low tide, we noticed that the boat was beached and a man was trying to push it into the water. We went over to help but his boat was firmly stuck in the mud. We invited the man to join us for dinner. He had fallen asleep as the tide was going out and woke up with his boat high and dry. After dinner the tide had come in enough so he could drive his boat away.

We also had an issue with our boat, but not because we fell asleep. The throttle kept getting stuck in neutral. We went into town to visit our friends at the outboard motor shop. We started to feel like we were their best customers. They knew what caused our problem so we bought the replacement parts and spent the next seven and one-half hours fixing it in the pouring rain.

The rain continued for several days in a row, yet it didn't stop us from counting otters throughout the northeastern part of the sound. We discovered that they traveled from bay to bay in groups. When the counts of otters were low in Nelson Bay, they were high in Simpson Bay and Orca Inlet. We also noticed that certain tagged individuals traveled together.

On July 5 we stayed in the trailer in Cordova. I called home and found out that my father did not have diverticulitis. He was now told that he had a different infection and was on antibiotics. He had lost a lot of weight and was very tired. I urged him to see another doctor.

Turk called Don and found out that he had received another $4,000 grant for our research. We were ecstatic! This would allow us to conduct more aerial counts over a wider area than we could survey in the boat.

A few days later we traveled through Orca Inlet to Hawkins Cutoff to observe otters hauled out on the mud. We were getting a lot better at navigating our way though the channel, and on the way there we were proud that we cruised along without getting stuck. The trickiest part was finding a way to get to land so we could do observations with the telescope. We had found that walking on the mud was difficult, and in fact, it was downright dangerous—a bit like quicksand. We eventually found a rocky area where we could safely get out of the boat and climb up a cliff. We saw 320 otters hauled out on the mud—the largest group yet! Most of the otters lay with their heads facing the water and they dashed back into the water at the slightest noise. In fact, as were driving toward the land to find a safe place to get out, they bolted back into the water en masse, flippers slapping in the sticky mud. However, in just a few minutes they all hauled out again. It seemed odd to be so skittish on land. They have no terrestrial predators, other than man, and in this area very few men were terrestrial—everyone was in a boat.

Only three otters rested on their backs on the mud, the others were on their stomachs. This was just the opposite from their resting position in the water, where they are always on their backs. Another difference was in their interactions. As individual otters climbed onto the mud bar they would go up to a hauled out otter and sniff. The hauled out otter sniffed back but there was no tumbling or wrestling. If they had, they would have become covered in mud.

Only 11 percent of these otters had white heads, which meant that this group was mainly younger otters. The group included several of our research otters from Nelson Bay.

All in all, it was a perfect day until the way back. Just as we were becoming confident that we could stay within the channel through the mud bars, we hit mud again. However, we were going quite slowly and did not damage the prop or motor, and did not get stuck. It just brought us back to the reality of always being a step away from disaster.

As we traveled through Orca Inlet we visually identified many of our otters from Nelson Bay and found that most of them had malfunctioning transmitters. In fact, when we got back to town, we tallied up the numbers and discovered that there were only four working transmitters, one of which had a very odd signal that indicated it was about to fail. Also, some of the transmitters that we had put in a bucket of salt water at camp developed the weird signal. We packaged up all of our remaining transmitters and mailed them back to the manufacturer so they could figure out why they were failing. We were starting to panic thinking that there wouldn't be enough time to get a new batch of working, reliable, transmitters before heading to Green Island. Meanwhile, we had lost a lot of valuable data on the Nelson Bay otters.

Since there were now few otters to radiotrack, we did a lot more feeding observations. This was quite time-consuming. Sometimes it took over three hours to collect a half hour of data. We would only use the data if we saw an otter feed for a full half hour. Many otters swam out of sight or quit feeding before the half hour was complete.

The following day we chartered a floatplane to fly us around the eastern part of Prince William Sound to count the otters in each of the bays. The pilot was actually waiting for us when we arrived at Chitina Air. Thank goodness he did not have a hangover this time. However, halfway through the flight the pilot landed the plane in a bay and said, "You don't mind if I check my crab pots, do you?" I guess that was better than flying with a toothache!

We conducted these flights in mid-morning when nearly all of the otters were resting so we could get an accurate count. Besides, since they rested in groups, they were easy to spot. For the larger groups we circled several times and both of us made independent counts. We also took photographs so we could later verify these counts by projecting the slides on the wall. On this day the water was calm, and it was overcast, so there was no glare—perfect conditions to count otters. We counted 810 otters.

In the afternoon, Dick took us out in a boat to pull his crab pots. The regulations allowed only male Dungeness crabs to be harvested for subsistence. The gender can be identified by flipping the crab over and looking at the bottom shell. Males have a mark that looks like an upside down "V." Females have a much wider mark. We caught and kept twenty-six males from only two pots. Dick showed us how to clean them. He grabbed both sets of legs and used the edge of the boat to pry off the top shell. Then he broke the crab in half and shook out the guts. Lastly, he removed the gills and soft tissue. We pitched in and cleaned the rest of the crabs and then went back to Dick's house for a wonderful feast with Kay.

The weather continued to rain every day. Salmon swam up the stream at our camp and we worried that bears would be attracted to them and become a nuisance around our camp.

On July 31 we did feeding observations for several hours. We saw Kate, the tagged female, and her pup. The pup was not yet big enough to swim. Males kept nuzzling Kate's groin as she was feeding but she disregarded them. We also saw an otter come to the surface with two Dungeness crabs in one-half hour. The otter took eight minutes to eat one of them and twelve minutes to eat the other. One crab was so large that the otter put a piece of the crab in the water and let it float while the otter ate the rest of the crab. In order to separate the top and bottom shells of the crab, the otter held the crab in its forepaws and pulled the top shell off with its teeth, much like we did against the edge of the boat.

We wanted to measure the depth of the feeding area where the otter captured the Dungeness crabs but we did not have our sounding rope with the rusty hammer in the boat. We tied a rock on the end of a heavy string and dropped it in the water. The string was ninety feet long and could not reach the bottom, so we dropped the anchor line and it, too, was too short. We tied the string to the anchor line and then lowered it back into the water, but the string broke, so we lost both the anchor and its line along with the heavy string. I guess not all of our decisions were better this year.

We received five transmitters in the mail that we had sent to the manufacturer. There was a note in the box stating that they were fixed. The note ended with, "Good luck." We wondered if the manufacturer thought, but did not write, "You'll need it." We decided to allocate some of the transmitters that were planned for use at Green Island to Nelson Bay otters, to make up for the transmitters that malfunctioned.

On August 1 we put one net into the water. When we got back to camp a bear had bitten into two containers of two-cycle oil and oil was leaking all over the ground. I knew we had it too good up to this point. Later, when we checked the net, we had a fifty-one-pound male and, as usual, it was PAR when we worked him up. We kidded each other saying that we did our best work in the rain. One of the modifications that we had made for this year was a way of recording the data during a hard rain. Turk had learned that divers use a Plexiglas slate to write on underwater. It was too expensive to buy an official diving slate, so he bought a piece of Plexiglas and roughed it up on a sanding belt so we could write on it with a pencil. Afterwards, we copied the notes to official data sheets in the tent and erased the notes on the slate using powdered cleanser. It worked great.

The next day we saw three otters that we had captured on Green Island the previous year in one of the rafts in Nelson Bay. One of them was Duke, whom we hadn't seen since he left his territory last September. We wondered if the three Green Island otters made the trip together since we had seen several traveling in groups. These sorts of discoveries kept us energized.

Later, when we were radiotracking, a boat from the Department of Transportation raced up to us and told me to call home immediately. We quickly drove to Cordova as I had a pit in my stomach. When I called my mother, she said my father was in the hospital and probably had lymphoma, a type of cancer. I made plans to fly to Florida to see him at the end of the week. When we got back to Nelson Bay, we had another otter in the net. We mechanically processed him, but my father's grave illness weighed on both of us.

We continued to count otters in all the bays in the eastern part of the sound. As we reviewed the data from the past year we noted seasonal shifts in their distribution that were the same for both years. In spring and summer many otters were in Nelson Bay. In mid-August a lot of them went into the back of Simpson Bay, and in winter many went to Orca Inlet.

One day we were doing feeding observations from some large rocks thirty feet above the surface of the water. Turk was looking through the telescope while I was recording the data. I thought I heard some small rocks rolling down the cliff in front of us. Before I had time to think about it, a black face appeared a few feet in front of us at the edge of the cliff. My first thought was that it was someone's dog, but then reality struck. I yelled, "Bear!" and it stopped and stared at us. Instinctually, we both grabbed a handful of pebbles, the only thing that was within reach, and threw them at the bear. He seemed as surprised as us and ran up the rocks into the woods. Afterwards we wondered why a bear would be climbing from the water up that cliff. Was it a coincidence or was he coming to investigate us? Thinking back on the episode that evening, we agreed that it was not a coincidence and we needed to be more diligent about keeping the rifle with us.

The next day we drove to Cordova and called the transmitter manufacturer to ask if they had found out the cause of the malfunctions. We called from a phone booth in the middle of town. It was pouring rain outside and drizzling rain inside the phone booth. We had a bad phone connection and there was an incredible amount of traffic noise on the street, including a large delivery truck, parked nearby, with the engine running, and exhaust coming into the phone booth. Turk struggled through the conversation and learned that the epoxy on the original transmitters had air pockets embedded in it that caused condensation to build up on some of the electronic components. This, in turn, caused corrosion and eventual failure of the transmitter. The engineers felt bad about this problem and made us twenty more transmitters, cast in a different material, and said they would ship them to us right away. We were optimistic that the transmitters would work much better on Green Island. As we walked down to the dock and got into the boat, Turk commented, "At least that's what I think they said. I could hardly hear anything."

# Torrential Rain

August 4 began as a bright, sunny day, ideal for radiotracking and feeding observations. In the late afternoon, we set up our telescope on some rocks in the middle of Nelson Bay. We were watching a large white-headed male diving for clams when all of a sudden a strong wind came across the bay, nearly knocking us off the rocks. Initially, we thought this was just a weird gust of wind coming off the mountains, but it didn't quit. One of us held the tripod while the other quickly dismantled the telescope before it blew over, and put it in its case. We rushed down to the boat, which was banging into the rocks. We didn't want to have another incident like Green Island where our boat blew away. This rock that we were on would be the worst place for that to happen. The bay turned from glassy flat to whitecaps in all directions, as if someone had just flipped a switch on a movie set. As we fought through the waves and slowly worked our way back to camp, we swung by the net and found that we had caught an otter. Bouncing around in the wind, we worked up the fifty-nine-pound male and made it back to camp at 8:30 PM, by which time it was raining steadily.

The heavy rain and wind did not let up, and limited what we could do. We worked up an otter at noon on August 6 but then spent the afternoon in the tent because the rain was coming down in torrents. When we came out of the tent in the early evening to check the net, our stream looked like a whitewater river. Turk and

I tried to cross it to get to the boat mooring. We held hands, but we couldn't do it. The force of the rushing water on our legs was too great, so we devised another plan. We tied one end of a rope on a large fallen tree on our side of the stream and the other end around Turk's waist so he would not be washed out into the bay as he attempted to cross. However, the force of the water was still too strong, and Turk retreated back.

We worried that our boat was full of water. We also worried about otters being caught in the net and not being able to get to them. In desperation, we looked around camp for items to make a raft; but then re-examining the situation we realized that even if we made a raft, the current would push us far out into Nelson Bay. Besides, from last year's experience on Green Island, Turk was still a little "raft shy."

As we walked along the side of the stream looking for a way to cross, we saw two partially eaten salmon high on the riverbank, clearly the work of a bear. We decided that *if* we made it to the boat we would stay in Cordova in the trailer from now on. The bears were too close for comfort.

Unable to find a way to cross the stream, we gave up and went to bed at 10:30 PM. All night we heard avalanches of rocks and trees tumbling down the side of the mountain. We worried that a rock or tree would come crashing into our tent. We occasionally poked our head outside and shined a flashlight around, but it was eerily dark and we couldn't tell what was happening. We tried getting some sleep, but it seemed that just as we faded off, there would be a loud thud near the tent.

We got up at 4:00 AM having given up on sleep. At 6:30 AM we walked outside and saw several two-foot diameter chunks of ice strewn all around the tent. They had cracked off from the glacier above the stream and hurled down the mountain, coming to rest on the only level ground. Suddenly, the idyllic camping spot at the foot of a waterfall appeared like a death trap. Amazingly, none of the chunks of ice hit our tent. The bears now seemed to be a minor issue.

We walked along the side of the stream and saw our boat in the distance, bobbing on the mooring with the back end underwater.

All the drugs for trapping were kept in a waterproof container in the back of the boat, and we had the sick feeling that they had floated out to sea. We had to push that thought aside, however, and deal with the imminent problem of crossing the stream to get to the boat.

We thought that the best chance of getting to the boat was to build a bridge across the stream. There was a tree trapped in the middle of the stream that had been ripped off the mountainside during the night. We looked around for some boards to nail together so we could put one end on the bank of the stream and the other end on the tree. After attaching two long boards together, the two of us held one end and attempted to guide the other end out to the tree. However, it was too heavy to hold and the far end dipped down, touched the water, got jerked from our hands, and was swept away in the current.

At that point we talked about calling the Coast Guard, but wondered if they would not view this as a true emergency. I looked down the stream and suggested that we make one last attempt to cross at a shallower area where the water wouldn't be so forceful. We took the rope that we had used unsuccessfully to cross the night before and tied it to a log on shore. I wrapped it around my waist, and Turk slowly fed out the other end, keeping tension on the rope. I walked very slowly and carefully chose each step. Halfway across the stream I was knocked down to my knees. I quickly stood up and took two more steps onto a shallower gravel bar. The rope wasn't long enough for me to travel any further, so Turk untied the rope from the log and followed me holding on to his end. At this point we had clearly thrown caution to the wind, but we were determined to get to the boat. Turk reached me three-fourths of the way across the stream. We held hands and took one small step at a time. The current, which was right up to the top of our hip boots, pushed hard against us and we had to lean into it to keep from being washed away. After taking several tiny steps, we finally made it to the other side of the stream. Jumping for joy in the pouring rain and howling wind, we then went to pull in the boat. We hoped that the rope wouldn't be twisted, requiring another swim. We pulled, and at first it felt stuck, but then we realized that the boat was just weighted down by the water—the back end was totally submerged. Once the boat was near shore, we bailed it out and found the drug container caught on some wires in the back! Just like last year's fortuitous snagging of the anchor when our boat was drifting out to sea without us, here again, a lucky snag saved us.

The boat started right away, a small miracle, so we sped out to the net. As we approached, we saw a black blob and were panic stricken at losing another otter. When we got closer, though, we were relieved to find that it was just a log. We untangled it, hauled the net into the bow of the boat, and drove to shore. We landed on the tent side of the stream and lugged the net high onto the beach. We were chilled and wet and decided we needed some hot chocolate and dry clothes before abandoning camp. We pulled the anchor line up the beach and hooked the anchor securely in the rocks because the tide was coming in.

On the way to the tent we went to get the cooler of food that we kept in the stream tied to a large tree, but the cooler—and the tree—were gone. The force of the raging stream, now river, had taken them out to sea. We realized that the tent, perched perilously on this small shelf of land, could be washed away as well. After quickly eating and changing clothes we packed up the necessary and valuable items at camp, stuffed them in red plastic bags, and put them in the boat to take to Cordova.

The rain hurt our faces and hands as it beat against us during the boat ride to town. It was also very foggy and we could hardly see the shoreline. The water got rougher as we rounded the point heading toward Cordova, and we had to slow way down.

Once in Cordova, we unloaded the boat and put some of the gear in a warehouse at the dock. We took a taxi to our trailer. The taxi driver told us that many places in Cordova were flooded.

That evening we decided to eat at the Reluctant Fisherman coffee shop because we were supposed to meet two marine biologists who had flown in from California. They did not show up at the Reluctant Fisherman, however, so we went to every hotel in Cordova looking for them, although we did not even know what they looked like. At one point, we asked a man in a bar who was playing pool if he was one of the people we were looking for because he seemed to match the description that we were given by Don. He was drunk and let us know he was not the guy we were looking for, but asked if we were up for a game of pool. When we got back to our trailer, we were surprised to find the biologists there, sleeping. None of the hotels in town had vacancies so they had called Don, who told them about our trailer, and suggested they call Dick. Dick told them where it was located so they found it, went inside, and crashed for the night.

The biologists were supposed to meet Ancel and his wife, Barb, in town the next morning. Ancel and Barb were at Olsen Bay and were going to come to town to pick them up. The weather was so bad we figured they would not be able to make the trip. We went to a local airline to ask if they could send a floatplane out to pick up Ancel and Barb because we thought they were stranded. But the pilot said it was too dangerous to fly. We walked back to town and suddenly saw Ancel and Barb. They had managed to make it despite the very rough seas. We also ran into Dick. He said he had asked the Alaska Department of Fish and Game to come get us at camp but they were too busy with other emergencies. Dick said he had never seen Cordova this flooded. We found out that it had rained sixteen and one-half inches on one day, and over forty inches (new record) the past five days. So far in August it had rained more than sixty inches. The record rains were discussed on *Good Morning America* and a local shop in town sold t-shirts proclaiming, "I survived the rains of 1981." What a great time to be doing sea otter research!

The following day we helped Ancel take gas barrels to Olsen Bay and we stayed there overnight. We could not get back to Cordova until the next evening due to rough water, rain, and fog.

On August 10 we checked the automatic tracking station in Nelson Bay and found that it had stopped working several days before. This was disappointing and very frustrating as it would have been interesting to find out what the otters did during the big storm. We half-joked about pitching the whole contraption into the ocean, and saying that it had been washed away in the storm. But, we shook it off, and after a half hour of work, got it running again.

We then went to our camp. The stream was totally transformed after the flash flooding. It was much wider below the waterfall and was divided into three parts, separated by two new gravel bars. A large chunk of the grassy knoll where our tent was located was washed away, as were a few trees. This made us realize how fragile and dynamic the shoreline was, which explained why all the vegetation at this site was so young.

The next week I flew to Florida to visit my father. He did have lymphoma and was going to start chemotherapy. Ancel sent his assistant, Jerry, from Anchorage, to help Turk with the study while I was away.

# Another Fishery Bites the Dust

On August 22 we packed the boat with gear from camp and took it to store at the Olsen Bay warehouse. We had mixed feelings about "closing up shop" at Nelson Bay. We knew we would never camp here again and there is always some sadness about doing something for the last time. However, we looked forward to the more remote, but comfortable field conditions at Green Island, as well as observing the interesting activities associated with the breeding season.

Later in the day we had time to do some feeding observations in Orca Inlet. We watched an otter feed for half an hour on large clams. At ten inches long they were the biggest clams we had ever seen. The otter sucked at the neck (siphon) of the clam and ate a huge chunk of it. Then he tried to pry open the shells, but was unsuccessful, so he sucked again and got the rest of the clam in his mouth. It took over three minutes for the otter to eat the whole clam. Other otters were also feeding on large clams and some of them banged the clams on a rock on their chests to open the shells. We saw a white-headed otter steal a clam from a smaller dark-headed otter. Looking closely, it became apparent that these otters were eating two different types of very large clams, one narrow and one more round.

We stopped into the Alaska Department of Fish and Game office to ask Al if he could identify the large clams that the otters were eating. We described them, and Al indicated that they were horse clams and razor clams. Razor clams weigh over one-quarter pound. He was particularly surprised that the otters would be eating either of these two types of clams because they have long siphons and are, therefore, very deep in the mud. Also, razor clams, which are long and narrow like a barber's straightedge razor, are noted for digging very quickly when the substrate is disturbed. Therefore, as an otter dug toward it, the clam would dig deeper. Al leaned back on his chair and muttered, "Your sea otters are going to destroy another shellfishery." And they did.

The next day we conducted an aerial survey of northeast Prince William Sound from a floatplane for over two hours. We counted nearly eight hundred otters, two hundred of which were in Orca Inlet. It was amazing how consistent our counts were, the total for the area never varied by more than twenty otters.

Over the next few days we radiotracked, did feeding observations from several sites, took down the automatic tracking station in Nelson Bay, and bought supplies for Green Island. We decided to take a lot of our gear to Chitina Air to fly out to us on Green Island. We did not want to travel in an overloaded boat again.

Priding ourselves on being more safety conscious with regard to the boat, the unexpected happened again. On the way to do feeding observations in Orca Inlet, the boat suddenly slowed down and we thought that, once again, we had hit a mud bar. It then suddenly sped up. A few minutes later, it did the same thing again. We checked the depth of the water and found that we were in the channel. This occurred several more times throughout the day. Back in town, we ran into Dick and he suggested that we check for water in the gas cans. We purchased a small hand-crank pump, specifically designed for this purpose. It had a long tube that reached the bottom of the can where any water would settle. We cranked the pump, and indeed found a fair amount of dirty water in the bottom of the cans. From then on we checked for water in every gas can before using it in the boat. This solved our problem. Dick came through again! It was nice not to have to worry about this knowing we were heading for Green Island.

We were still anxiously waiting for the new transmitters, hoping we would get them before going to Green Island. We checked the post office every day, but they did not arrive. We decided we would go to Green Island, anyway, and have Chitina Air check our mail over the next few days and bring us the transmitters when they brought out our gear. If they didn't arrive by the day they were going to fly out with our gear, we would have them delivered on the mail run.

The next day we packed for Green Island, looking forward to the final segment of our field research. However, we were uneasy about leaving without having the transmitters, the key component of our study, in hand. We hoped that these would not suffer the same fate as the tent poles that were mailed via UPS last year.

# Breeding Season on Green Island

On August 27 we loaded the boat with all our red bags to go to Green Island. Al had informed us of a weather station on Hinchinbrook Island so we called before leaving Cordova and found out that the water across the Hinchinbrook Entrance was very rough. By 11:00 AM things seemed to be calming down so we decided to leave, but were forced to turn back before we got to Simpson Bay due to the high waves with whitecaps. We called the station again at 4:00 PM and they told us the water was "like a mill pond" so we headed out. As we left the Cordova harbor we saw a sea otter eating clams by one of the anchored boats. Their boldness was not going to help their reputation. We were able to drive within ten feet of it.

The water across the mouth of Simpson Bay was a little rough but it flattened out by the time we got to the Hinchinbrook Entrance. However, when we got to Montague Island, we had five-foot seas, and we went up and down them like a roller coaster. It took us an hour to get to Green Island from there, normally a half hour trip. During the last half hour three different groups of Dall's porpoises chased our boat. They came within two feet of the front of the boat. They surfaced, blew air, and then dove down in the water over and over again. We arrived at Green Island at 7:15 PM, a three and one-quarter hour trip—our longest yet.

We spent the evening unpacking and settling into the cabin,

which had the feeling of being "home." We also set a mooring for the boat. We took our binoculars and scanned around for Otto, but didn't see him. It was dark by 9:00 PM and we knew we would drastically lose daylight hours over the next six weeks.

The following day the floatplane arrived with our gear, but no transmitters! They had even checked the post office right before they flew out to us. After this disappointment, we spent many hours observing sea otters. We saw two territorial males. We watched one of these males feeding with a female and pup in the back of Camp Cove. We were disappointed that it was not Otto. We noticed that the female had total control of the diving sequence. When she finished consuming her food on the surface and dove, the male would immediately follow her even if he hadn't finished eating. Often, the male had to discard his last clam or two because the female was already finished with her food, usually because she had given some to her pup. The pup, meanwhile, generally dove with the female but never came up with any food. We wondered what the pup was doing underwater. Could it see the mother digging? This was doubtful because a lot of silt would have been stirred up while she dug in the mud making it impossible to see. Did the pup even make it to the bottom?

Two days later we radioed the boat, the *Montague*, because they were bringing oil for our stove to Montague Island and we had to go meet them. The water was choppy so they came a little closer to Green Island. We drove out to them and the captain, Harry, used a winch to place two fifty-five-gallon drums of stove oil into our boat. We used Harry's radio to contact Chitina Air to find out if our transmitters had arrived—they had not. We slowly drove the boat back to Green Island, pushed the drums into the water, and rolled them up the beach and into the shed. By now, we had become very good at this.

While we were waiting for the transmitters we could not do any trapping so we spent most of our time doing feeding observations, counting and identifying otters in the anchorage, and monitoring their behavior. We were able to identify several females that we had caught last year. We saw one female still with her pup from last year and she even gave it some food on several dives. Her year-old pup frequently surfaced from a dive without any food. This female must not have had a new pup this year. We also saw other females who had pups last year without any pups this year. These observations led us to believe that females often give birth every other year.

It was obvious that otters at Green Island did not have the same activity patterns as the otters in the male area. Otters here did not raft together early in the morning and they appeared to eat most of the day. This must be due to the poorer food supply at Green Island. Both the clams and crabs were much smaller here.

The next morning we radioed the Fish and Wildlife Service office in Anchorage and left a message for Ancel to call Don in Minnesota to track down the transmitters. If they were lost in the mail our whole study was in jeopardy.

We decided to build a "portable blind" so we could observe the otters from land without being seen by them. We had noticed last year that our presence on the beach disrupted some of their behaviors. We made the blind using four pieces of plywood, three sides and a top. We put it together with nuts and bolts so it could easily be dismantled, moved around in the boat, and quickly reassembled. A second major advantage of this blind was protection from the rain.

In our first use of the blind we saw a dark-headed male breed with a white-headed female. The male was smaller than the female and could not reach her nose to bite and hold on during the copulation so he bit the back of the female's neck instead! This was the first time we saw a non-territorial male actually breed.

Later, we observed a female drifting out of a male's territory on her back and the male swam next to her on his stomach, put his head on her head, and nudged her back into his area. When she drifted away again, he grabbed her with his forepaws. Was she just pretending to be asleep and teasing or testing him? The female made subtle vocalizations, the same that we heard last year when females were with males during the breeding season.

On September 1 the water was calm, so we took advantage of the conditions and did a complete count of otters around Green Island, Channel Island, Little Green Island, and Barrier Island (fig. 3). We counted eighty-five adult otters and eight pups. Ancel did a count in the spring of this year and counted ninety otters. We saw three separate groups of otters resting and eating in kelp (*Nereocystis*) beds. A highlight of the day was a brief beach-combing excursion on Channel Island. From a distance, Channel Island is the shape and size of an oil tanker—there is a pinnacle of rocks at one end, and the rest is a long, flat, bar. The gravel beach collects an assortment of driftwood and discarded or lost items from boats. I had specifically been hoping to find a round, glass, float used by Japanese fishermen. However, they were extremely rare and we had never seen one in any of our previous days of walking the beach. However, luck was with us, and on this day we were thrilled to find two of them!

That night we received a call on the radio stating that the transmitters were tracked to the Cordova post office, and Chitina Air would bring them to us the next day on the mail run. What a relief! On this day we had made a count of otters in a large area, found two Japanese floats, and learned that our transmitters were on the way—we were flying high!

The floatplane arrived the next afternoon and delivered the transmitters along with our groceries and mail. We painted the transmitters and set two capture nets. That night as we were writing our field notes, we heard a crackling sound on the radio and it sounded like someone said something about Green Island. We answered back, asking if someone was trying to reach us. The voice at the other end was Cal, from the Fish and Wildlife Service in Anchorage, inquiring if we got the transmitters. He also said he would monitor the radio every night at 9:00 PM in case we needed anything. The camaraderie of the people in Alaska never ceased to amaze us!

Over the next several days we saw another tagged territorial male. This male was caught on Green Island last year, was seen in Nelson Bay this past August, and was now back on Green Island again. We also saw an otter that was caught in Nelson Bay earlier this year. We were astounded by the distances that otters traveled in Prince William Sound.

Although our observations were going well, trapping was not. We had one stretch of eleven days without catching any otters.

We spent a lot of our time trying to catch Big Brute, who appeared to be the king pin of the anchorage. He seemed to be very aware of the net and casually dove under it whenever he was near it, almost showing off in front of us. We decided it was time to try the dart gun. On our first attempt, Brute was swimming near the end of the spit and Turk got off a shot, but it landed too far in front of Brute. We then devised a second plan. I would try to direct Brute toward shore by slowly approaching him in the boat while Turk would be waiting on land with the gun. We attempted this on several occasions but Brute would either swim off in the wrong direction, or just dive and come up far out of range. On one day, however, things seemed to be working as planned. Brute was swimming slowly on his back, intently watching me in the boat, as he moved closer to where Turk was waiting on shore. Turk pumped up the gun and got ready to shoot. When Brute was thirty feet away from Turk, he took a shot. The dart flew out, but the wind caused it to veer to the right, so it missed Brute. He quickly dove underwater. I directed him toward shore one more time. This time he swam even closer. Turk took another shot. At the sound of the shot Brute flinched and pulled his hips underwater, just in time to avoid the dart. Reminiscent of last year when we were trying to catch Otto in Camp Cove, we were hell-bent on catching Brute.

The weather was progressively deteriorating and we knew that we could not continue to trap much longer. In the early morning of September 29, it was pouring rain and very cold. Standing on the beach in front of the cabin we could see some black blobs in one of the nets in Camp Cove. Turk looked with the binoculars and said it looked like we had a harbor seal and a log. We rowed out to the Whaler and bilged out several inches of water in the back of the boat. We drove out to the net, not happy about the prospect of having to untangle another harbor seal. When we got to the net, the blobs turned out to be three otters, a large male and a female and pup caught in the same spot. The male and female were fighting and the pup was not moving. We separated the male and female and drugged them. The pup had drowned and we pulled it into the boat. It was a twenty-pound pup that we had caught only three weeks earlier. Then we pulled the male and female into the boat. The male had a small laceration on his lower jaw from fighting in the net. When we checked his flippers there were holes from previous tags that Ancel had put on him several years before, identifying him as Brute. This was a bittersweet moment—catching a prized territorial male on the last day of trapping, just like last year, but losing a pup in the process. The female had a bloody nose, but was otherwise in good health. She was the exact same weight, forty-six pounds, as she was three weeks before.

When we were working on these otters, another large male swam by and got caught in the far end of the same net! Was he sensing that Brute was gone and he could take over his territory? This otter weighed eighty pounds, five pounds less than Brute.

After working up the otters we drove up to the last net, hoping it would be empty. We had not eaten breakfast yet, had worked up three otters in the pouring rain, and were feeling bad about the dead pup, whom we had gotten to know during the previous weeks. Unfortunately, as we approached this net, we saw a giant mess. There were three harbor seals caught in same spot. The net was extremely tangled and it was very difficult to free the harbor seals. We were both lying on our stomachs leaning over the bow with our hands in the cold water trying to pull pieces of net over the flippers and heads of the struggling seals. Each time we made a little headway, the seals would thrash and splash and get more tangled. We were at our wits end and it was probably good that no one else heard the things we said to the seals. We were eventually able to free two of them while they were in the water, but we had to pull the net into the boat to untangle the third one. The harbor seal went wild, thrashing around on the bow and struggling to bite us when we tried to free it. We used the pocketknife liberally on the net. This seal had such a foul odor we had to scrub the boat after it was released in order to get rid of the stench.

It took us four hours to work up the otters and release the harbor seals. Our bodies were shivering in the cold, our hands were frozen, and we were more than ready for some hot oatmeal with raisins.

We were finally finished with trapping. We had caught six females with pups, eight solitary females, one solitary pup, four males, and six harbor seals. Three of the males were territorial males from last year. One of these we named "Walter" in honor of my father. We named the last big male who tried to sneak into Brute's territory, "Ivan," after Turk's father.

We learned a lot about territorial males from our daily observations. All but one of the territorial males that we had seen last year were back in their territories by September 5. Otto never came back. We thought he may have died over the winter, but hoped that he had just found a better territory somewhere else, without a more dominant male (Brute) blocking the entrance and intercepting many of the females.

Territorial males often left their territories during the day to feed but always returned at night. During the evening hours they swam the perimeter of their territory on their backs while they groomed their chests—the territorial patrol. Males frequently rested on a border of their territory, probably so they could attract females as they swam by, keep females inside from leaving, and prevent other males from entering. Territorial males never rested near each other.

We wondered why it was so important to protect a territory at night and not during the day. We learned that the otter population was higher in the anchorage at night. Several of the otters that we were tracking routinely moved out of the anchorage during the day, but returned at night to rest in protected bays. That also explained why, at Green Island, we captured more otters at night.

We learned the exact territories of seven different males (fig. 4). Some stayed in the same territory the whole time we were at Green Island. Others stayed in their territories and bred with several females for a month or so, and then left. As soon as a male left his territory, another male took his place. Non-territorial males swam through the anchorage frequently checking to see if there were any open territories. One of these, Ivan, the last male that we caught, hung around outside of Gibbon Anchorage but never found a territory.

Breeding pairs usually stayed together for two- to two and one-half days—the same as we observed last year. Males and females had repeated copulations that lasted over twenty minutes each.

However, on the last day before the female left the territory, they did not copulate, but just fed and rested together. It appeared that the male wanted to make sure the female was no longer in estrus before allowing her to leave his territory.

The day after we caught Brute fighting with the female, they were together as a "mated pair." How quickly they made up from their scuffle in the net, and she had moved on from the loss of her pup. She had a fresh nose scar from breeding and we saw them copulate many more times. The following day Brute stayed very close to her but they did not mate. The next day Brute did not stay with the female but he did not let her leave his territory for two more days! Any time she tried to swim out he blocked the exit.

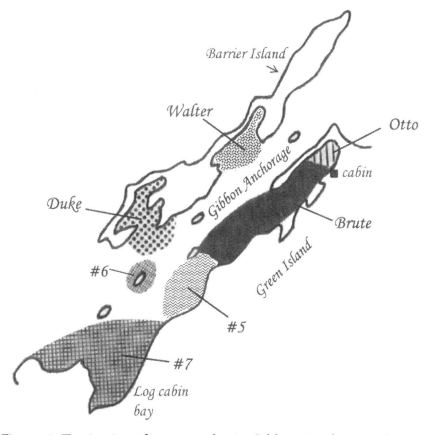

Figure 4. Territories of seven males in Gibbon Anchorage. Some territorial boundaries and males changed during the study e.g., Otto.

146

Sometimes a male would approach a female and she would just swim away without any interaction. Other times we saw shorter copulations of one to ten minutes, after which the female would leave the area. They did not become a mated pair and stay together. It is unclear why males allowed some females to leave, while they invested more time in others.

As we observed last year, males bred with females who had a pup. This led us to believe that many females must have pups every year. We noticed that the mating sequence with a female still attended by a pup often required more than three days. This was probably due to the fact that the pup frequently interfered with the male-female interactions, which prevented prolonged and frequent copulations.

We observed some territorial males use force with females. One male aggressively pushed a female with his forepaws back into his territory as she was trying to escape.

Another female was hauled out on the beach and a male hauled out just above her and used his forepaws to push her toward the water. They both went into the water. A few hours later we saw a fresh nose scar on her and when she was feeding near the male she made a cooing sound. The male followed her to the back of the bay and they copulated for twenty-eight minutes. A few hours later Turk was walking on the beach, coming back from the tracking station, and the female was hauled out again. The male was resting in the water five feet from shore. I was further down the beach and hollered to Turk. The male hauled out quickly, stepped over the female and started looking around (as if he were protecting her). The female started cooing and touched the male with her forepaws. This obviously excited him. He pushed her toward the water with his forepaws. They both went in the water and copulated again.

A different male and female that were together for almost three days as a mated pair totally ignored each other when they were feeding in the same bay three days later. It appeared that the male was no longer exerting any influence over her and their relationship was over. For some reason she remained in his territory. She was obviously no longer in estrus.

Another male that had been with a female for three days kept a close watch on the female during day four and would not allow her to leave his territory. He did not swim or feed next to her, however, when she attempted to leave his territory he swam ahead of her, turned on his back, and groomed his chest. It appeared like he cut her off so she could not leave. She turned around and continued feeding in his territory. Two days later he totally ignored her and she was free to go. We wondered if he stayed with her until she was fully out of estrus to assure that she did not breed with any other male.

There seemed to be several clear benefits for a male otter to have a territory in a protected bay: 1) the bay offered a calm resting area, which attracted females particularly during the stormy weather, 2) the bays had shallow feeding areas that attracted females with pups, and 3) the landforms surrounding the bays provided impenetrable borders making it easier for the males to prevent other males from entering and females from leaving. This is why Gibbon Anchorage, with all of its islands and inlets was an ideal breeding area.

Sometimes we saw females copulate with non-territorial males. However, they did not stay with the males and become mated pairs. Although we never saw a female breed with more than one male, we could not keep perfect track of all the females after they mated, especially those without transmitters. We presumed that some of the females that mated with non-territorial males might have mated with multiple males—otherwise, territorial males would not have invested so much time in making sure that females were out of estrus before they could leave their territory. Thus, while some males could successfully breed without a territory they were probably less likely to sire offspring.

We watched pups grow, learn to swim, and learn to dive for food. We observed constant improvement in their success rates in coming to the surface with food. Initially, they often surfaced with no food, then sometimes came up with large empty clamshells, and eventually started obtaining live clams. Pups frequently climbed on their mothers for food even when they were old enough to successfully forage themselves. One time we saw a female surface with a large sea star, a non-preferred food. She ate off the legs and gave the body to her pup. The pup immediately threw it in the water without eating it.

We saw pups disperse from their mothers when they were five- to six-months-old and weighed approximately thirty pounds. However, nearly all of the dispersed pups that we monitored died. It appeared that the food supply around Gibbon Anchorage was inadequate for independent pups, who were limited to feeding in fairly shallow water. In this small population, it appeared that it would have been more beneficial for the female to keep the pup for a longer period of time. As it was, the six months of dedicated nurturing was all for naught. In the one case where we saw a female taking care of her one-year-old pup, we wondered if the pup had left and then reunited with its mother, or if the pup had never dispersed.

We also saw two sick females separate from their pups when they were clearly too young to survive. One female had been caught in the net with her pup and we noticed that the female's chest was enlarged. The next day we saw them both hauled out on the beach and the pup appeared to be energetic and healthy. However, two days later, the female was hauled out without her pup. Her chest was even larger. The following day she was in the water lying on her back with her eyes closed doing slow log rolls, and the next day we found her dead on the beach. On the necropsy her left lung was filled with air bubbles, indicative of pneumonia. We saw the pup alive two days later (four days after being separated from its mother) only two hundred yards from where its mother died. We do not understand what kept the pup away from its sick mother, but we presume it had something to do with her abnormal behavior. Since the pup was only eighteen pounds and we never saw it forage successfully, we assumed it eventually died. Unfortunately, we could not determine its fate because it only had flipper tags and no transmitter. The remarkable thing about this story is that we likely would not have seen this pup alive after the mother died had it not been for a fluke occurrence. The anchor dragged on one of our nets and it drifted away. We happened to see this pup as we were searching for the net.

A second premature separation of a female and pup occurred

two weeks later. The female had a very small pup, which was alive the day before they separated. When Turk observed them that day, the pup was on the mother's chest, and both seemed sluggish. Since pups often sleep on their mother's chest, they can appear very still. On the other hand, mothers have been known to carry around dead pups. Later that day I went back to watch the pair again, and saw the pup swimming beside its mother. The next day the female was alone and she hauled out of the water frequently, was very thin, and had a swollen chest. Her pup was definitely too small to survive on its own. We watched her for several days. Twelve days after she was hauled out on the beach we saw her feeding normally. She was even in a bay with a territorial male but she did not mate with him. The following spring Ancel saw this female with another pup. In this case, the apparent abandonment of the pup enabled her to survive and reproduce again. Of note, Turk witnessed a third case of abandonment the next year.

There appeared to be several distinct reasons for otters to haul out. Hauling out is clearly an energy saving behavior. All of the sick otters hauled out. Females also hauled out after copulating. This may have served two purposes: to regain their energy, and to preclude the male from copulating with them again until they were ready. (Otters only copulated in the water). Females with pups seemed to haul out more than lone females, probably due to the high energetic demands of raising a pup. During the spring through fall we only saw adult males at Green Island haul out if they were with a female. However, Turk saw them haul out in the winter when the water was colder and often rougher. We can't explain why males at Green Island uncommonly hauled out, whereas the males in Orca Inlet did so on a daily basis. We suspected that the otters in Orca Inlet felt less threatened because they were in large groups.

Hauling out obviously entails some risks because otters are very clumsy on land. Somewhat like a seal, they rested no more than a few yards from the water. They appeared nervous on land and frequently ran back into the water when we drove by in the boat. The males in Orca Inlet probably felt more comfortable in having the safety of numbers so they could sleep knowing that other companions were watching.

Whenever we saw otters on land we would later return to the spot to collect fresh scats. The scats contained shells from clams, cockles, mussels, and crabs.

This year, we were determined to get better information on how much time otters spent feeding versus resting and the time of day these activities occurred. Last year the tracking station on Green Island did not work as well as we had hoped. To remedy this, we brought equipment to boost the radio signal that was received at the tracking station on the cliff. We also brought equipment for a second tracking station.

The problem with the station on the cliff was that the cable carrying the signal from the antennas to the receiver was so long that it weakened the signal, which made it insufficient to trigger the recorder. We brought a pre-amp to increase the signal strength. However, it would have to be connected at the top of the cable, which meant that Turk would have to climb the tree again. We picked out a sunny day to do this. Turk had a high-energy breakfast and psyched himself up for the climb. As he began the climb I told him when he got to the spot where he had to jump, he needed to take some time and reassess the risk versus the benefit of collecting the data. The pre-amp required the power of a car battery to run and, therefore, had two long cables that would reach from the top of the tree to the battery on the ground. I watched the cables unwind on the ground as Turk climbed the tree. When the cables were three-fourths of the way unwound, they stopped moving for several minutes. I kept quiet and thought Turk might actually consider abandoning the operation, but then the cables started moving up again. After twenty minutes he shouted down, "Give it a try." I connected the pre-amp cables to the battery and in just a few seconds the ink pens started clicking away. I hollered up to him, "Mission accomplished!" When Turk was finally safely on the ground he said, "Okay, that is really the last time that I will climb that sucker!"

Later that day, we picked out a spot on Island Four to set up the second tracking station. Fortunately, the trees were much smaller and the climb was relatively easy for Turk. This station was helpful in collecting activity data on otters at the south end of Gibbon Anchorage.

Although it appeared that the tracking stations were working well, we were intent on corroborating the data with first hand information. During the daytime we could compare visual observations with the station data, and at night Turk often radiotracked from the blind. It was important to be able to differentiate on the tracking station recordings, signals from feeding otters, which cut out when the otter was submerged, versus signals of otters that were far away from the station and could only be picked up intermittently. Therefore, we radiotracked from the boat and attempted to obtain daily locations on all the otters. By the combination of all these methods we obtained highly reliable twenty-four-hour data.

Acquiring this data required a grueling schedule. Turk often tracked all night from the blind, I would then pick him up and drop him off at the cabin, and then I would radiotrack the rest of the day. One morning I picked him up and we saw some otters interacting in Camp Cove. I slowed down the boat and we both grabbed our binoculars. One of the lens caps on Turk's binoculars flew into the water. Turk was so tired that when he bent over to get it he just fell in. Luckily, he was wearing his float coat, which made him very buoyant. Although the water temperature was very cold, he was able to climb right back into the boat. We both laughed. The situation was more humorous than dangerous and was obviously the result of being sleep deprived.

Although we were engrossed in the data collection, we took advantage of the benefits of living on the ocean. Harry, the captain of the *Montague*, told us about a great spot to catch shrimp. We found a shrimp pot in the shed and took it to this area and baited it with raw hamburger. One week later we pulled up the pot and only had two shrimp, two small crabs, and two whelks (similar to snails). We tried again, this time baiting the pot with fish heads, and when we pulled it up a week later we had twenty-six shrimp. The third time we baited the pot we could not pull it up for ten days because the water was too rough to get out there. When we were finally able to drive out to pull it up we were led by a convoy of Dall's porpoises. In the pot were twenty shrimp, one crab, and one fish. We ended up with some fabulous meals.

We also put out a crab pot, but not to catch dinner. We needed to collect some Helmet crabs to bring back to Minnesota to analyze for their caloric value. We also needed to collect various sizes and types of clams and mussels for the same reason. In the process, though, we collected extra to make clam chowder.

During observations one day we found huckleberries in the woods and picked enough to make a cobbler for dessert. I checked them carefully for worms before cooking with them.

The wildlife all around us was always spectacular. If we had not been so totally preoccupied with the otters, it would have been easy to get distracted watching all the birds. We saw tufted and horn puffins, pigeon guillemots, harlequin ducks, oystercatchers, auklets, murrelets, yellowlegs, plovers, sandpipers, loons, murres, Barrow's golden eye, bald eagles, and our friends, the Steller's jays. I fed the Steller's jays bread almost every day. In fact, whenever we opened the cabin door to go outside the jays would squawk at us to give them some food! Sometimes one jay would see me place bread on the ground and then call to the others to come and eat. By the end of October we had six Steller's jays near the cabin.

The number of harbor seals increased dramatically in Camp Cove. We noticed this last year and figured it must be their breeding season, too. In fact, in September and October the harbor seals floated differently in the water. Normally, only their heads were visible, however, this time of year they floated with their heads and hind ends out of the water!

One night we heard on the radio that subsistence fishing for razor clams and Dungeness crabs in Orca Inlet was closed due to the low populations of each species. This was the first time in Alaska that subsistence fishing was banned! We knew that people in Cordova would be very angry at "our" sea otters.

Everything was going pretty smoothly when one day, near the end of September we were driving the boat and felt the steering wheel slipping to the right. We knew right away from our previous experience what was wrong. Turk took apart the steering linkage, greased all the parts, and reassembled it, but it did not work any better. We called the U.S. Fish and Wildlife Service in Anchorage on the radio and they told Ancel about our problem. Ancel bought the parts for us and shipped them to Chitina Air in Cordova so they could fly them out to us on the next mail flight. When Chitina Air came to Green Island the next day, however, they did not have the parts for the boat. We radioed the U.S. Fish and Wildlife Service that night and they said they would check on it for us. The next night we received a northwind stating that the parts would be flown out to us the next day. They did not arrive the next day and that night we got another northwind stating that a different airline was doing the mail flights, and our parts would be brought over to that airline and flown out to us the next day. The plane actually came the next day and we fixed the boat.

Similar to last year, it rained almost every day. Instead of our outside "rain showers," we figured out a way to take a bath in the cabin. There was a large metal tub outside so we brought it into the cabin, heated water on the oil stove, and filled the tub. We took turns being the first one to get to bathe in the water. The second person had to wash with the "used" water.

In late September we had our first morning frost, and the boat had a layer of ice on it. On September 30 we saw snow on the mountains on Knight Island and five days later we saw snow on the mountains on Montague Island. On some clear, cold nights we saw amazing northern lights. Usually it started with a faint glow across the horizon, which would broaden to a wide band, with vertical streaks. The lights would change shape and fade in and out like a shimmering curtain. Generally, they were pale yellow or green, but occasionally we saw orange streaks. We often sat outside and watched them for a half hour or more.

We recognized that this was a very special place and we were very lucky to be here. However, it became difficult to keep that in mind as the weather got progressively colder and rainier.

# Cabin Fever

The weather deteriorated significantly from late September to the end of October making data collection more and more difficult. Compounding that, the hours of daylight decreased dramatically each day. Instead of being able to do observations during the evening hours, we were forced to spend more time in the cabin.

We spent a lot of time writing field notes and tabulating data, but we also found ourselves with a little free time. One night, with the rain pounding on the tin roof, we came up with a bowling game to stave off cabin fever. We set up cans of WD-40 oil and insect repellent as bowling pins and used a softball that we had found on the beach as a bowling ball. It became our nightly recreation.

We also liked to listen to the radio even though it only received one station that came in very weak and with a lot of static. One night we heard that the local grocery store in Cordova, named ACC, had a meat slogan contest and the winner would receive four large steaks. For the next few days it became our mission to come up with a winning slogan. Turk never liked any of mine and I never liked his. Nevertheless, one day when the plane came to deliver our mail and groceries I gave the pilot a letter to mail to ACC with my entry to the contest—"You'll have no beef when you steak your trust in ACC." Two weeks later we heard through the crackle on the radio that I won the contest! I mailed a letter to Dick and Kay telling them that they could have the meat.

We also looked forward to a radio show on Friday nights called, "Desperate and Dateless." It was a live call-in show where two people, either two men or two women, were on separate phone lines and a third person of the opposite sex would call in. The person calling in would ask personal questions to the other two, but the other two could not hear each other's responses. The caller would then choose one of them for a date. Oftentimes it did appear that the people were desperate for a date, and I guess we, as listeners, had become desperate for entertainment.

# Stranded on Green Island

By mid-October we had a long stretch of days with pouring rain and strong winds. One day, in the third week of October, there was an unusually high tide, so we decided to take the boat out of the water. We pulled it up as high as we could on shore and rested it on logs on the beach. We cleaned it after the tide went out and kept it stored there for Ancel's next visit to Green Island. We put a 15-hp motor on the rowboat to use for radiotracking until we left the island.

A biologist from California flew to Green Island to study mussels for a week, and he had arranged for a floatplane to pick him up on October 21. The weather was really bad and the plane never came. We had arranged for a floatplane to pick us up on October 22. We were totally packed, closed down the cabin, and a floatplane came at 3:00 PM. The pilot said he did not have room for the three of us, so Turk and I stayed back. The pilot said he would call another plane to get us. We sat on the beach for hours, but no plane ever came. On October 23 we, again, waited all day, but no plane came. We received a northwind that night saying that the pilot was waiting for good weather before he would pick us up. This was certainly a setback given how ready we were to leave, but we used the extra time to collect more data.

The next morning thick clouds hung just above the water and we knew a plane would not make it out to us. However, by noon a breeze came up and it soon became clear and sunny. We could not stray from the cabin because we did not know if and when the plane might arrive. We were fortunate that Brute and a female that had abandoned her pup were feeding in front of the cabin so we continued to gather some interesting information. At 3:00 PM we heard a plane overhead and we rushed into the cabin to once again haul our gear down to the beach. However, the sound of the plane trailed off into the distance and never came back. My heart just sank. We radioed the Coast Guard and they said that Cordova was fogged in and many planes could not fly. We started talking about how long we could be stranded and wondered if our food supply would last. We did not have any fresh food and only had a little canned food left. By this time I was feeling pretty bummed. Turk said it would make a good book if we got stuck here for a month. I told him I thought we already had enough adventures for a book.

On the morning of October 25 we awoke at daylight and, again, hauled all of our gear down to the beach. A plane arrived at 7:15 AM and we were ecstatic! Fortunately, the weather was so good we could also conduct an aerial survey of sea otters in the northeastern sound on the way back to Cordova. We counted 813 sea otters plus two pups. This was remarkably similar to our past counts of this area.

When we got to Cordova we saw Dick in town and he invited us to dinner. He had picked up the steaks that I won from the meat slogan contest and saved them for us. As usual, we had a great evening with Dick and Kay and, although we were leaving, we knew they would be lifelong friends.

When we got back to the trailer after dinner, we found it had run out of gas so there was no heat. How ironic that our study began and ended with problems with the trailer. We were really cold and shivered in our sleeping bags. We eventually took the sleeping bags into the Forest Service warehouse and slept on the cement floor. The next day we finished packing and flew out of Cordova. Our final field season was over.

# Reflections

When Turk told me I would have a lot of firsts if I married him, I never imagined we would experience so many adventures in Alaska. Prince William Sound is an incredibly beautiful place and we often felt like we were the only two people in the world. We were totally engrossed in the study—it was amazing to watch otters on a daily basis and learn about their social relationships, feeding, activity patterns, and breeding. We felt that we got to know them as individuals, with distinct personalities. We had daily discussions about our observations and continually developed theories, only to have many of them negated as we collected more data. We both loved studying sea otters and I felt like it was my study as much as it was Turk's PhD project. Turk always treated me as an equal partner and researcher.

We learned to solve many problems as they occurred, and we realized that our minds had a synergistic effect when brainstorming solutions or developing theories about our findings. That synergism has carried forth to the present day, in many different life situations. Although we took a bit of a risk testing a young marriage in such strenuous, unforgiving, wearing, and intense conditions, we both felt that we grew together as a couple. We also found it gratifying that we not only learned an enormous amount, but we made a significant contribution to science.

Our study would not have been feasible without the support

of Ancel Johnson, Don Siniff, Dick Groff, and many people from the U.S. Forest Service, and the Alaska Department of Fish and Game. Everyone recognized there were risks involved in working out of a small boat in the ocean, living alone in a tent camp or on an uninhabited island, and they did whatever they could to help us. This study was a once in a lifetime experience for both of us (a first and a last?), and Prince William Sound will always have a special place in our hearts.

# Major Findings of Our Study

## Movements

Sea otters in Prince William Sound were generally segregated by gender until the breeding season in September and October. Even then, a small proportion of males left the male areas to attempt to breed in the female areas. Breeding males made seasonal movements of over sixty miles but often would return to the male areas in just a few weeks. A smaller number of males remained in the distant female areas for several months.

Males in northeastern Prince William Sound lived together in big bays and frequently rested in large groups (rafts) of fifty to several hundred otters. We presumed that these rafts afforded them more protection from predators. (In recent times, their main predator was man, who hunted them for about 150 years). They broke off from the rafts to feed, individually, usually in the same bay that they were resting.

As males diminished their food supply in one area, they moved into an adjacent, unoccupied bay. This is the process by which the population expanded. We witnessed the expansion of this population into the last unoccupied portion of northeastern Prince William Sound (Orca Inlet).

Home ranges of sea otters are comprised of a set of heavily used areas interconnected by travel routes. When males were in Nelson Bay they used areas of four to five square miles. When they moved to a different bay, they often traveled in groups, and some of these companionships were maintained for several weeks even as they moved about the various bays. They easily traveled at speeds of more than three miles an hour and had excellent homing abilities (as was evident when we moved them to different bays).

Some of the bay-to-bay movements by males were influenced by boat traffic associated with the various commercial fishing seasons. For example, the number of otters in Orca Inlet ranged from an average of fifty during the peak of the salmon fishing season to over five hundred when fishing was closed.

After males vacated a bay, some exploratory females moved in, and then it evolved into a female area. Once it became a female area, it remained so. Green Island had been a female area several decades prior to our study.

While raising pups, females frequented shallow protected bays in order to teach their pups to forage and also to protect them from stormy seas. Many of these shallow bays did not have a good food supply so females moved to better, deeper, foraging areas after separating from their pup. Similarly, many males who had territories in these shallow areas left on a daily basis to feed in better foraging areas. In summary, movements of sea otters were influenced by breeding, pup rearing, food supply, and availability of sites to escape stormy seas.

## Feeding

We observed and timed over twelve hundred foraging dives. Clams comprised 85% of the diet in Nelson Bay and 97% in Orca Inlet. The remainder of the diet in these areas was large Dungeness crabs and a few fat innkeepers. The diet was much more diverse at Green Island. There, clams were still the principal food (76%) but otters also ate a lot of small crabs (13%) and mussels (6%), plus occasional fat innkeepers, worms, sea stars, sea urchins, and kelp.

Adult otters were highly successful at foraging in all areas. They came up with food on 80–95% of their foraging dives. However, otters in the male area obtained either more food items or larger food items per dive than they did at Green Island (which explains why they traveled back to the male area after breeding). Because of this, otters in the male area fed an average of only 8.8 hours per day compared to 11.5 hours at Green Island. Caloric intake for body weight averaged the same in the two areas, although otters at Green Island invested more energy foraging to obtain those calories.

Balancing caloric intake and energy expended was most difficult for females with pups. They not only had to nurse their pup and give away much of their food, they had to feed in areas dictated by their pup's limited diving ability. As such, they spent almost thirteen hours a day feeding in shallow areas on generally small food items. Consequently, it was labor-intensive for females to be able to find enough food for themselves and their pups, and this took a toll on their health.

Young, dispersed pups had the most difficult time finding sufficient food. They fed mainly on mussels, eating shell and all. This satiated them, but did not provide enough calories to sustain them. Nearly every pup that we monitored through independence died before its first birthday.

## Activity patterns

In both Nelson Bay and at Green Island nearly all otters could be found feeding shortly after sunrise. One to two hours later, otters at Nelson Bay began resting and continued to do so until late afternoon, at which time some of them began feeding again. Most feeding in this area occurred at night, coinciding with the time that Dungeness crabs, their preferred prey, were most active and, therefore, most vulnerable to capture. Nearly the opposite activity pattern occurred at Green Island, where most of the feeding occurred during the day and otters rested most of the night.

In the spring and summer when the weather tended to be warmer and the seas calmer, Green Island otters also took a long nap during the day. As the weather conditions deteriorated in the fall and winter, they rested less. Even in Nelson Bay we noticed that poor weather conditions delayed the daily raft formation or caused the rafts to split up earlier than usual. It was clear that otters, just like us, liked to bask in the (rare) sun. They fanned out their flippers to absorb the heat and were reluctant to get their flippers wet even when another otter or a human intruder disturbed them.

## Breeding

Mating occurred year round but peaked in September and October. Females first bred at four-years-old and were capable of pupping annually, although not all did so. Females either separated from their pups before breeding, or bred while with their pups.

Large male otters (seventy to ninety pounds), established territories in female areas. These territories, which were usually defined by land forms such as coves or islands, enabled them to consort and breed with several females, keep other males away, and discourage females from leaving until they were out of estrus. Males mated with multiple females in succession, but did not tend more than one female at a time. Male mating success was related to his age and weight, quality of his territory, and the length of time he occupied his territory.

Some copulations, particularly short ones, occurred between females and non-territorial males. Afterwards, the male and female went their separate ways. Breeding between females and territorial males was a more prolonged affair and we presume more successful in conception. Typically, a territorial male and lone estrus female stayed together for two to three days. On the first day the male tended the female by swimming close to her, feeding when she fed, and diving synchronously with her. Then they would copulate multiple times for twenty to forty minutes each time. On day two, the male stayed very close to the female but usually did not breed. The female typically left the territory on day three, although sometimes the male would not let her leave, even though he did not copulate with her or tend to her. We presume that he kept her from leaving until she was fully out of estrus, as we never observed a female with a second male.

Territorial males also consorted with females that still had their pups. The frequent interactions between the male and female sometimes prompted the separation of her and the pup. If a pup remained with the female, the mating process lasted several more days. This was due to the pup physically interfering with the mating activity, and also possibly affecting the hormonal state of the mother.

## Raising pups

In Prince William Sound, pups were usually born in May or June, but some pupping occurred through August, or rarely later. Females had only one pup at a time. Pups weighed three to four pounds at birth and nursed until they were able to obtain food on their own. Pup rearing was a very demanding activity. Females taught their pups to swim, dive, and forage for food. Females moved into shallow protected bays when they had young pups to provide them easier access to food and protection from rough water.

Some sick females abandoned their pups when they were too young to survive on their own. Abandonment reduced the burden on a sick female and may have enabled her to recover. In our study, one sick female that abandoned her pup died and another regained health and had a pup the following year. In 1982, while Turk was experimenting with a different transmitter attachment, he witnessed this again and both the mother and pup died.

Pups separated from their mothers when they weighed approximately thirty pounds. Female offspring stayed in the same general area that their mother used to raise them. Young males dispersed to male areas and stayed there until they were old enough to breed.

## Conflicts with fishermen

The Dungeness crab fishing season was closed in 1980 after sea otters moved into the last unoccupied areas of northeastern Prince William Sound and virtually depleted the harvestable crab population. Similarly, the commercial and subsistence fishery for razor clams closed in 1981, the year after large numbers of sea otters inhabited Orca Inlet. We saw otters eat, on average, twelve crabs and over eighty clams daily, and the otter population in northeast Prince William Sound ranged between four hundred and nine hundred otters. This number of otters eating that number of crabs and clams obviously had a big impact on populations of these shellfish. As a result, we saw a dramatic shift in the attitude of both the commercial crab fishermen and the local public toward sea otters from 1980 to 1981.

Fishermen felt sea otters were enjoyable to watch and did not detract from their livelihoods when we interviewed them during the first year of our study. After the crab fishery was closed in 1980, boat traffic lessened, and even more otters were attracted to Nelson Bay and Orca Inlet. Since otters eat resting on their backs, and spend several minutes eating a crab, they are highly visible. Seeing hundreds of otters gobbling up crabs was like being slapped in the face to the commercial crab fishermen. By 1981 most fishermen no longer derived any enjoyment from seeing sea otters, they felt there were far too many, and they wanted a hunting season to reduce their numbers. Local residents generally felt much the same way. We were very fortunate that the timing of our study was such that we could witness the rapid and large-scale effects that otters could have on their prey populations. To this day, the commercial crab and razor clam fisheries have remained closed.

## Methodological Improvements

We caught over one hundred sea otters during our study. The capture method and the drug protocol that we used were highly effective and are still used to this day. However, there are several shortfalls in the use of the capture nets. First, when multiple otters are caught in the same spot in the net they tend to fight and injure each other. Second, non-target species, such as harbor seals, are often caught. And third, it is difficult to capture specific individuals. Our experiments with the dart gun to target specific individuals proved ineffective and researchers today have still not succeeded with that technique. However, some researchers have been able to capture otters using diver-held traps that are pushed to the surface from underwater. Other researchers have been able to capture pups (while the mother is underwater) using hand-held dip nets from a boat.

Although the flipper-mounted transmitters provided us with a wealth of information that could not have been obtained any other way, they were far from ideal. The electronic components often malfunctioned, otters chewed off the antennas, and most otters were able to remove them from their flippers within three months. As a result, the year after this study Turk and Don conducted experiments with transmitters that were surgically implanted into the abdomen. The signal was weaker than the flipper transmitters, which made the range much shorter. However, the implanted transmitters worked consistently for over a year. The electronic components are much more reliable because they are not exposed to the environmental elements or biting by the sea otter. These implanted transmitters have no detrimental effects on the health or reproduction of the otters and are widely used today.

The tracking station that we used, which functioned using ink and chart paper, provided over seventeen thousand otter-hours of activity data and was vital to our study. However, it frequently malfunctioned. Moreover, Turk had to spend three months reading and interpreting the recorded blips on hundreds of yards of paper, record the information on data sheets, and then type it all into a computer. Today, researchers use pressure-sensitive implanted transmitters that record the time and depth of every dive that an otter makes. Hence, if the otter can be recaptured and the transmitter extracted, a researcher can obtain a complete digital record of foraging activity. The advantages of our now obsolete method, was that it did not require capturing and handling the otters more than once, did not have the risk of surgery, and enabled us to determine the amount of time otters spent resting and swimming, as well as feeding. With all the frustrations (and dangers) of setting up the antennas, jiggling the recorder to get it to work, checking the station daily in the most bug and bear-infested areas, I never thought I would be ending this book touting the benefits of this technique!

# Publications from Our Study

Garshelis, D. L. 1983. Ecology of sea otters in Prince William Sound, Alaska. PhD diss., University of Minnesota.

Garshelis, D. L. 1984. Age estimation of living sea otters. *Journal of Wildlife Management* 48:456–463.

Garshelis, D. L., and J. A. Garshelis. 1984. Movements and management of sea otters in Alaska. *Journal of Wildlife Management* 48(3): 665–678.

Garshelis, D. L., and J. A. Garshelis. 1987. Atypical pup rearing strategies by sea otters. *Marine Mammal Science* 3(3): 263–270.

Garshelis, D. L., A. M. Johnson, and J. A. Garshelis. 1984. Social organization of sea otters in Prince William Sound, Alaska. *Canadian Journal of Zoology* 62:2648–2658.

Garshelis, D. L., J. A. Garshelis and A. T. Kimker. 1986. Sea otter time budgets and prey relationships in Alaska. *Journal of Wildlife Management* 50:637–647.

Garshelis, D. L, and D. B. Siniff. 1983. Evaluation of radio-transmitter attachments for sea otters. *Wildlife Society Bulletin* 11:378–383.

# About the Author

Judy Garshelis lived in a remote tent camp and on an uninhabited island in Prince William Sound, Alaska, while assisting her husband with his PhD research study of sea otters. That experience led her to write this book. She also coauthored, with her husband, four scientific articles that were published in professional journals.

Presently, Judy works as a family nurse practitioner in northern Minnesota. She previously worked as a hospital nurse, public health nurse, perinatal nurse specialist, and director of a maternal and child health program. She published the results of her Master's research, authored a perinatal newsletter, and has written and received several grants for her work in public health.

Judy received her Bachelor's degree in nursing from the University of Vermont, her Master's degree in public health from the University of Minnesota, and her Master's degree in nursing from the College of St. Scholastica, Minnesota. She lives in a small, rural Minnesota town with her husband (their two sons are grown and live elsewhere). She enjoys the outdoors, particularly water skiing in the summer and downhill and x-country skiing in the winter. She also periodically returns to Alaska to revisit her favorite otters.

Breinigsville, PA USA
23 September 2009
224556BV00001B/4/P